Our choice:

INTRODUCTION

Time for Food guides are designed to help you find interesting and enjoyable places to eat in the world's main tourist destinations. Each guide divides the destination into eight areas. Each area has a map, followed by a selection of the restaurants, cafés, bars, pubs and food markets in that area. The aim is to cover the whole spectrum of food establishments, from gourmet temples to humble cafés, plus good food shops or delicatessens where you can buy picnic ingredients or food to cook yourself.

If you are looking for a particular restaurant, regardless of its location, or a particular type of cuisine, you can turn to the Food Finder, starting on page 4. This lists all the establishments reviewed in this guide by name (in alphabetical order) and then by cuisine type.

PRICES

Unlike some guides, we have not wasted space telling you how bad a restaurant is – bad or poor-value restaurants simply do not make it into the guide. Many other guides ask restaurants to pay for their entries, or expect the restaurant to advertise in return for a listing. We do neither of these things: the restaurants and cafés featured here simply represent a selection of places that the authors have sampled and enjoyed.

If there is one consistent criterion for inclusion in the guide, it is good value. Good value does not, of course,

mean cheap necessarily. Food lovers know the difference between a restaurant where the high prices are fully justified by the quality of the ingredients and the excellence of the cooking and presentation of the food, and meretricious establishments where high prices are merely the result of pretentious attitudes.

Some of the restaurants featured here are undeniably expensive if you consume caviar and champagne, but even haute cuisine establishments offer set-price menus (especially at lunchtime) allowing budget diners to enjoy dishes created by top chefs and every bit as good as those on the regular menu. At the same time, some of the eating places listed here might not make it into more conventional food guides, because they are relatively humble cafés or takeaways. Some are deliberately oriented towards tourists, but there is nothing wrong in that: what some guides dismiss as 'tourist traps' may be deservedly popular for providing choice and good value.

FEEDBACK

You may or may not agree with the authors' choice – in either case we would like to know about your experiences. Any feedback you give us and any recommendations you make will be followed up, so that you can look forward to seeing your restaurant suggestions in print in the next edition.

Feedback forms have been included at the back of the book and you can e-mail us with comments by writing to: *timeforfood@thomascook.com*. No food guide can keep pace with the changing restaurant scene, as chefs move on, establishments open or close, and menus, opening hours or credit card details change. Let us know what you like or do not like about the restaurants featured here. Tell us if you discover shops, pubs, cafés, bars, restaurants or markets that

you think should go in the guide. Let us know if you discover changes – say to telephone numbers or opening times.

Symbols used in this guide

VISA	Visa accepted
Diners Club	Diners Club accepted
MasterCard	MasterCard accepted
Restaurant	Restaurant
Bar	Bar, café or pub
Shop	Shop, market or picnic site
Ø	Telephone
Transport	Transport
2	Numbered red circles relate to the maps at the start of the section

The price indications used in this guide have the following meanings:

❻	budget level
❻❻	typical/average for the destination
❻❻❻	up-market

FOOD FINDER

Celetná

Eateries in this area cluster around the Ungelt, the beautiful complex of buildings behind the Týn Church, renovated only a few years ago. The fashionable avenue known as Pařížská leads to the Jewish Quarter which now boasts a quality kosher restaurant, King Solomon.

Letenské sady

nábřeží Edvarda Beneše

N

J

Dvořákovo nábřeží

SYNAGOGUES

Pařížská

Bílk

3

26 16

17 listo padů

19

39 15 4

Široká

30

38

Maiselova

20

Křižovnická

M

Valentinská

Kaprova

Platnéřská

CELETNÁ
Restaurants

Alexander's ❶

Rybná 29

∅ 2481 4434

Ⓜ Metro Náměstí Republiky

Open: daily 1130–2400

Reservations recommended

All credit cards accepted

International

❶❶❶

Swedish chef, Lars Sjostrand, describes the menu at Alexander's as 'cosmopolitan'. Certainly all the dishes are prepared to a consistently high standard, and in line with the best practice of nouvelle cuisine (eg fresh produce). As a starter try the deep fried oyster skewers, or, if your tastebuds really need waking up, the grilled prawns cooked in a mouth-watering curry and chilli sauce.

Archiv ❷

Masná 3

∅ 2481 9297

Ⓜ Metro Náměstí Republiky

Open: daily 1200–2400

Reservations recommended

All credit cards accepted

French-International

❶❶–❶❶❶

This pleasant Old Town eatery occupies a late 19th-century building and has a small garden terrace. While not cheap, most of the nouvelle cuisine dishes more than pass muster. Try the stuffed quail or the duck salad with chestnuts to start, and the beef *à la mode* or *filet mignon* as a main course. A good wine list is on offer.

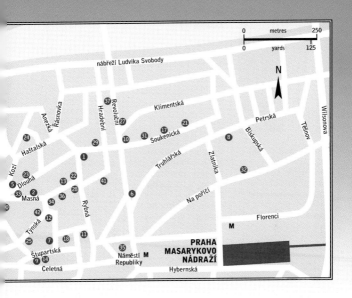

Jewel of India ❸

Pařížská 20

☎ 2481 1010

🅜 Metro Staroměstská

Open: daily 1200–1430, 1800–2300

Reservations recommended

All credit cards accepted

Indian

❶❷❸

This American-owned restaurant offers a creditable selection of Mughal (North Indian) dishes, including *machhi massala* (fish cooked in Indian spices), *rogan josh* (lamb curry) and *murgh tikka massala* (cubes of grilled chicken cooked in an onion sauce). There's the usual range of delicious Indian breads. One criticism – some of the curries are on the bland side – the *dhal* suffers most from this deficiency. In the daytime there's a special lunch menu; beware, the cost of an à la carte meal soon mounts up.

King Solomon ❹

Široká 8

☎ 2481 8752

🅜 Metro Staroměstská

Open: Mon–Thu, Sun 1100–2300, Fri 1100–90 min before Sabbath

Reservations recommended

All credit cards accepted

Jewish (Kosher)

❶❷❸

The main dining space of this new restaurant in the heart of the Jewish Quarter is divided into alcoves – ideal for business lunches or a

▲ Caprese salad

romantic meal. There's also a glass-roofed terrace in the courtyard. Many of the dishes are inspired by traditional Yiddish recipes, for example *gefilte* fish and *joych*-feast soup (chicken broth with almond drops).

Kozička ❺

Kozí 1

✆ 2481 8308

🚇 Metro Náměstí Republiky

Open: Mon–Fri 1200–0400,
Sat–Sun 1600–0400

Reservations essential

💳 VISA

International

❶❷

The setting is a converted coal cellar with bare brick walls. Not very salubrious you might think, but this busy eatery is a definite hit with the Czech diners who crowd in here each evening. One reason for its popularity is the meaty fare, with steaks, chops and beef dishes very much to the fore; the other is the excellent selection of wines: 160 vintages from around the world with a not unreasonable bias towards France.

Macao ❻

Truhlářská 3

✆ 231 6093

🚇 Metro Náměstí Republiky

Open: daily 1100–2300

Reservations recommended

💳 VISA

Chinese

❶❷

Handy if you've been shopping in the Kotva department store or staring open-mouthed at the glories of Obecní Dům, this standard Chinese restaurant offers the usual mix of meat and vegetable dishes, with equally predictable rice and noodle accompaniments. Despite the predominantly Czech clientele, the food is less bland than is often the case in Prague. Other plusses are the light, airy interior and the commendably unobtrusive service (English is spoken by at least one member of staff).

Metamorphosis ❼

Malá Štupartská 5

Týnský Dvůr

✆ 2482 7058

🚇 Metro Náměstí Republiky

Open: daily 1100–0100;
café from 0900 (1000 Sun)

Reservations recommended

All credit cards accepted

Italian-Czech

❶❷–❶❷❸

Enjoying a prized location in the beautifully restored Týn courtyard, Metamorphosis offers a two-in-one experience. Upstairs is the café, decorated in cheerful oranges and greens. The light meals served here include pasta and other Italian dishes, salads, filled baguettes and desserts (outside tables look out on to the Týn Church). The restaurant downstairs is in a renovated 17th-century cellar which makes the most of the original stone vaults. Live music in both dining areas starts daily from 2000.

U Petrské Věže ❽

Petrská 12

✆ 232 9856

🚇 Metro Náměstí Republiky

Open: Mon–Fri 1200–2400,
Sat–Sun 1800–0100

Reservations recommended

All credit cards accepted

Czech

❶❷❸

Every detail of the 'Peter's Tower' restaurant, from the stained-glass windows to the candelabra, gilt-framed mirrors and brocaded chairs, is calculated to suggest elegance and refinement. The kitchen is Czech but with a commendable dash of continental sophistication. Mushrooms stuffed with meat and tomatoes in red wine is the house speciality while the *pièce de résistance*, breast of wild duck with black sauce, made from dark beer, honey and nuts, is arguably unsurpassable.

La Provence ❾

Štupartská 9

☏ 9005 4510

📍 Metro Náměstí Republiky

Open: daily 0800–0100

Reservations recommended

All credit cards accepted

French

●●●

Very much the real McCoy, this French restaurant is in great demand. You enter via the *tapas* bar but downstairs is a world away – Provence in fact, at least that's what the rustic décor hints at. You could select almost anything from the menu and go home satisfied but the *cassoulet* and coq au vin take some beating. Not suitable for an intimate dinner – it's just too busy.

Řecká Taverna ⑩

Revoluční 16

☏ 231 7762

🚊 Trams 5, 14 and 26

Open: Mon–Fri 1000–2400, Sat–Sun 1100–2400

Reservations unnecessary

All credit cards accepted

Greek

●●

Decked out in the Greek national colours of blue and white, this typical taverna is a fount of unpretentious but sound cooking. All the Aegean favourites are here, from *tzatziki* and *dolmades* to *skordalia*, *souvlaki* and moussaka.

Red Hot & Blues ⑪

Jakubská 12

☏ 231 4639

📍 Metro Náměstí Republiky

Open: daily 0900–2300

Reservations recommended

All credit cards accepted

Mexican

●●

You'll find this survivor from the US migration of the early 1990s just behind the Kotva department store. Famously laid back, it remains a popular haven for ex-pats and English-speaking visitors. The food is Tex-Mex with a nod towards Cajun: shrimp gumbo, bean burritos, eggplant creole and *quesadillas*. There's live music every night and a courtyard for enjoying the sunshine.

Rybí Trh ⑫

Týnský dvůr 5

☏ 2489 5447

📍 Metro Náměstí Republiky

Open: daily 1100–2400

Reservations essential

All credit cards accepted

International-Fish

●●●

'The Fish Market' is situated in the delightful Týn courtyard, just behind the church. Freshwater and sea fish, shellfish and crustaceans are all flown in daily and laid out on beds of crushed ice for your inspection. You choose what you want then decide how you would like it cooked (stewed, roasted or grilled) – nothing could be simpler.

Zlatá Ulička ⑬

Masná 9

☏ 232 0884

📍 Metro Náměstí Republiky

Open: daily 1000–2400

Reservations recommended

No credit cards accepted

Yugoslav

●●

'Golden Lane' inspired both the name and the décor of this popular Yugoslav eatery – hence the backdrop of shingle roofs, cottage façades and birdcages. To eat pizzas here would be a bit of a waste. Concentrate instead on the traditional dishes, such as Serbian *shish* kebab.

▲ Rybí Trh

CELETNÁ
Bars, cafés and pubs

Banana Café 🄐

Štupartská 9

☎ 9005 4510

🄜 Metro Náměstí Republiky

Open: daily 1800–2000

💶

This lively night bar above **La Provence** restaurant (*see page 11*) recently celebrated its fifth anniversary and looks set to continue for another decade at least. The *tapas* bar is the focal point during the twilight hours, but once the night crowd spills out from the back room, the pumped-up dance music ends any hope of conversation.

Café Franz Kafka 🄑

Široká 12

☎ 231 8945

🄜 Metro Staroměstská

Open: daily 0800–2200

💶

While there's no obvious connection with the writer, this alluring moody coffee-house, decorated with sombre frescos, is a good spot for a light lunch.

Café Klub 🄒

Pařížská 18

∅ None available

🄜 Metro Staroměstská

Open: daily 0800–2200

💶

A glitzy café-bar in a smart shopping street, which doles out home-made bagels, pancakes, ice creams, strudels and light snacks.

Café Relax 🄓

Soukenická 7

☎ 2481 8892

🄜 Trams 5, 14 and 26

Open: Mon–Fri 1000–2300, Sat 1300–2300

💶

Behind a cluttered window display made

up of old typewriters, phonographs, sewing machines and other paraphernalia is a no-frills café-bar dispensing the cheapest Staropramen in Prague; also Rulanské and other Czech wines and a small selection of appetising snacks. The pool table is the main source of entertainment.

Chapeau Rouge 🄔

Jakubská 2

∅ None available

🄜 Metro Náměstí Republiky

Open: daily 1900–0500

💶

Chapeau Rouge is a lively late-night bar just across the road from St James's Church. At weekends at least, it's jam-packed with teenage tourists trying to make themselves heard above the thumping disco.

Dolce Vita 🄕

Široká 15

☎ 232 9192

🄜 Metro Staroměstská

Open: daily 0800–2400

💶💶

A good place to relax with a cappuccino and catch up on the news at home (foreign papers are available) ... or it could be, were it not for mobile phone addicts who tend to haunt the

place. The art-nouveau setting is lovely and the Italian-style snacks (mozzarella and tomato, and melons) are equally appealing.

U Golema 20

| Maislova 8 |
| Ø 232 8165 |
| Ⓜ Metro Staroměstská |
| Open: Mon–Fri 1100–2200, Sat 1100–2300 |

Ⓒ Ⓒ

As you might guess, this popular café-*vinárna* is located in the Jewish quarter. Open for lunch and dinner, the varied menu ranges from vegetarian risotto to fried carp or baked duck with dumplings and sauerkraut.

Góvinda Vegetarian Club 21

| Soukenická 27 |
| Ø None available |
| Ⓜ Trams 5, 14 and 26 |
| Open: Mon–Sat 1100–1700 |

Ⓒ

Run by a community of Hare Krishna, this cheerful cafeteria is a haven for vegetarians browned off with Prague *vinárnas*. The portions of rice-based dishes are large enough to satisfy the most voracious appetite.

Hostinec U Templáře 22

| Masná 17 |
| Ø None available |
| Ⓜ Metro Náměstí Republiky |
| Open: daily 1000–2200 |

Ⓒ

'At the Templars' is a large, smoky *pivnice*, serving up light and dark Czech beer, wines and spirits.

Inverhouse 23

| Dlouhá 31 |
| Ø 232 1575 |
| Ⓜ Metro Náměstí Republiky |
| Open: Mon–Fri 0900–0100, Sat–Sun 1800–0100 |

Ⓒ

This whisky drinkers' paradise, with an excellent selection of Scottish and Irish malts and bourbons, also rustles up a good breakfast: ham with horseradish and whipped cream, cakes, bread and marmalade.

Molly Malone's 24

| U obecního domu 4 |
| Ø 534 793 |
| Ⓜ Metro Náměstí Republiky |
| Open: Sun–Thu 1200–0100, Fri–Sat 1200–0200 |

Ⓒ

Typical 'Irish pub abroad' guaranteeing a warm welcome, cool Guinness and half a dozen food choices daily.

Týnská Literární Kavárna 25

| Týnská 8 |
| Ø 2482 7212 |
| Ⓜ Metro Náměstí Republiky |
| Open: Mon–Sat 0800–2300, Sun 1000–2300 |

Ⓒ

You could easily miss this warm friendly café near the Týn church – look out for the sign outside 'Dům U Zlatého Prstenu'. Students and other young people drop in throughout the day to browse in the small (Czech) bookshop or to listen to jazz in the evenings.

Valmont 26

| Pařížská 19 |
| Ø 232 7260 |
| Ⓜ Metro Staroměstská |
| Open: daily 0900–2400 |
| All credit cards accepted |

Ⓒ Ⓒ

A bustling pub-restaurant with a good line in steaks, Czech beers and Moravian wines. Other dishes include omelettes, tiger prawns in chilli mayonnaise, pork cutlets in port with beans, and duck with apples.

CELETNÁ
Shops, markets and picnic sites

Bakeries and confectioners

Cukrárna ㉗

Revoluční 12

🚇 Trams 5, 14 and 26

Open: Mon–Fri 0900–1900, Sat–Sun 1000–1900

This large, busy confectioners with limited seating, has an appetising selection of filled baguettes; also pre-wrapped sandwiches; cakes and pastries, chocolates, ice creams and drinks. There's also one novelty: 'Viagra here for sale without prescription'. Seeing is believing!

Cukrárna U Lucerny ㉘

Rybná corner of Masná

🚇 Metro Náměstí Republiky

Open: Mon–Fri 0800–1800, Sat–Sun 1100–1800

Typical Old Town confectioners, with a good line in pastries, creamy cakes and fancy biscuits. You'll also find a range of alcoholic and soft drinks as well as coffee and boxes of chocolates.

Michelské Pekárny ㉙

Dlouhá 1

🚇 Metro Náměstí Republiky

Open: Mon–Fri 0730–1800, Sat 0800–1400

Apart from an intriguing selection of Czech breads, this large bakery specialises in filled pastries, cakes, doughnuts and pancakes.

Pekařství ㉚

Široká 6

🚇 Metro Staroměstská

Open: Mon–Fri 0700–2000, Sat–Sun 1000–2030

You'll find this bakery and delicatessen in the heart of the Jewish quarter. Look out for the mouth-watering doughnuts and sugared pastries (you can eat on the premises if you wish). Other products include bread rolls, biscuits, crisps, sweets, wines and champagnes.

Grocers and supermarkets

České Kuře ㉛

Soukenická 3

🚇 Trams 5, 14 and 26

Open: Mon–Fri 0930–2000

A humble chicken grill for takeaways with a few tables to eat at.

Diskont Plus ㉜

Na poříčí 23

🚇 Metro Náměstí Republiky

Open: Mon–Fri 0800–1900, Sat 0800–1800

You'll find this useful supermarket in the Bílá Labut (White Swan) shopping centre.

Grilované kuře ㉝

Masná 1

🚇 Metro Náměstí Republiky

Open: daily 0800–2000

The name 'Grilled chicken' says it all. You can also buy bread rolls, Pepsi, Coca Cola and beers.

U Groše ㉞

Masná 20

🚇 Metro Náměstí Republiky

Open: Mon–Fri 0800–1800, Sat 1000–1800, Sun 1000–1800

Fast food counter selling filled rolls, sandwiches, sweets, drinks and hamburgers.

Julius Meinl ㉟

Náměstí Republiky 8

🚇 Metro Náměstí Republiky

Open: Mon–Fri 0700–2000, Sat 0800–1800, Sun 1000–2000

This branch of the well-known Austrian supermarket chain is just outside the metro station.

Neptun ㊱

Masná 20

🚇 Metro Náměstí Republiky

Open: Mon–Fri 0800–1800, Sat 0900–1200

A delicatessen with fishy overtones – the dish of the day might include carp. Also meat and vegetable salads.

Pasta Fresca ㊲

Revoluční 25

🚊 Trams 5, 14 and 26

Open: Mon–Fri 0730–1730, Sat 0900–1200

'Fresh pasta' is a take-away with an excellent range of salads as well as pasta dishes. There's also a small indoor eating area for those who want to stop for a light lunch.

Potraviny ㊳

Maislova 6

🅜 Metro Staroměstská

Open: Mon–Fri 0700–1830, Sat 700–1130

You'll find this large grocery store in the middle of the Jewish quarter. Specialities include chocolates and Becherovka liqueur.

Potraviny ㊴

Široká 16

🅜 Metro Staroměstská

Open: Mon–Fri 0630–1900, Sat 0700–1400, Sun 1200–1800

Well-stocked, western style supermarket, selling fresh bread and spirits, among other things, and novelty souvenirs such as Staropramen aprons.

Samoobsluha ㊵

Dlouhá 14

🅜 Metro Náměstí Republiky

Open: Mon–Fri 0600–1930, Sat 0700–1400, Sun 1000–1700

This small supermarket sells fresh bread and is a major outlet for Krušovice beer.

Žecnitstvy ㊶

Benediktská 6

🅜 Metro Náměstí Republiky

Open: Mon–Wed 0700–1800, Thu 0700–1900, Fri 0700–1830

This large delicatessen near Obecní Dům has an appetising array of salads, cheeses, meats and bread.

Wines

Wine Shop Ungelt ㊷

Týnský dvůr 7

🅜 Metro Náměstí Republiky

Open: daily 1100–2300

Tucked away in a medieval courtyard behind Týn Church is this useful store selling quality wines from around the world – including a Bordeaux from 1811. There are tastings daily in the historic brick-vaulted 14th-century cellar.

▲ Julius Meinl delicatessen

Czech cuisine and wines

Eat, drink and be merry!

Traditional Bohemian cooking owes a good deal to the cuisines of Central Europe: schnitzels and strudels from Austria, sauerkraut and dumplings from Germany, goulash and paprika from Hungary and sour cream and rissoles from Serbia. Like the Austrians, the Czechs take pride in the popular origins of their dishes – the recipes handed down from one generation to the next by the likes of **Magdalena Rettigová**, the Mrs Beaton of 19th-century Czech gastronomy. In our more health-conscious age these heavily meat-based dishes, high on fat and cholesterol, not to mention calories, get a predictably bad press. And while the more enterprising restaurateurs now offer somewhat lighter (and more enlightened) fare, many pubs and *vinárnas* adhere stubbornly to tradition.

Joints of pork, beef, and lamb, usually grilled or roasted, are invariably served in rich sweet or spicy gravies of wine, beer, or sautéed fruit. Poultry is often served stuffed with almonds, livers or even prawns. Game is excellent value and there's still plenty of it, despite the best efforts of Archduke Franz Ferdinand who, prior to his assassination in 1914, bagged more than 300,000 of the creatures on his estate at Konopiště. Wild boar, pheasant, quail, venison, roe deer, rabbit or hare – you can take your pick, but spare a thought for the poor Moravian sparrow! All main courses come with gargantuan helpings of roasted, boiled or creamed potatoes (chips are for wimps) and dumplings, *knedliky* in Czech.

If you're not a meat lover, the fish dishes may tempt you. The lakes and rivers of Bohemia and Moravia are rich in freshwater fish: carp, pike-perch, trout, sheat, and eel (salmon is imported). Common saltwater fish include halibut, turbot, mackerel and sole.

Dumplings crop up again on the dessert menu, this time filled with plums and other fruit, sprinkled with sugar and curd cheese and doused in melted butter. Strudels are also popular, served with vanilla ice cream or whipped cream, as are *palačinký*

▲ Sirloin of beef

– pancakes with jam or fruit filling, sometimes laced with chocolate sauce.

WINES

Wine was first cultivated in Roman times – in AD 276 the Roman legions of *Vindobona* (Vienna) planted vineyards in *Pálava* (Moravia). While modern Czech wines are inferior to those of Slovakia, many are pleasantly drinkable, the main problem being consistency. Good years include 1983, 1988, 1990–3 and 1997 (the wine of the century), but steer clear of the dreaded 1994–5 and 1998 vintages. If you're thinking of taking wine home with you (very little is produced for export) seek the advice of one of the specialist wine shops, otherwise, cast an eye over the shelves of the local supermarket – you'll find some real bargains.

▲ Czech wines

Most Czech wine comes from Moravia, roughly between Brno and the Austrian border. Major vineyards include Mikulov, Znojmo and Velké Pavlovice. Of the whites, the most common is the perky, highly palatable Rýnský Ryzlink (Rhenish Riesling). Rulandské Bílé (Pinot Blanc) improves with ageing, while creditable varieties of Chardonnay and Sauvignon are starting to make an appearance. Mention should also be made of Ryzling Vlašsky, used to make the eminently drinkable sparkling wine, Bohemia Sekt. Among the

> **Wild boar, pheasant, quail, venison, roe deer, rabbit or hare – you can take your pick, but spare a thought for the poor Moravian sparrow!**

red wines, many experts rate Rulandské Červené, a full-bodied number, not dissimilar to Burgundy. Running a close second is Portugalské Modré (Blue Portugal) from Kobylí. Frankovka and Vavřinecké/Svatovavřinecké are more commonplace, but serviceable.

BOHEMIAN WINE

Bohemian wine is produced in very small quantities owing to the poor growing conditions (mainly climatic). If you want to taste what you're missing, the pretty hilltop town of Mělník is only a short drive from Prague (half an hour by bus, leaving from Florenc coach station). The local wine is served in restaurants or you can take a tour of the chateau with tastings (✆ *0206 626853; open: May–Sept*) in the fabulous 13th-century wine cellars.

Karlova

Beneath the stunning baroque façades of the Old Town lie much older foundations. Many of these Gothic and Romanesque cellars now make attractive vinárnas (wine bar-restaurants).

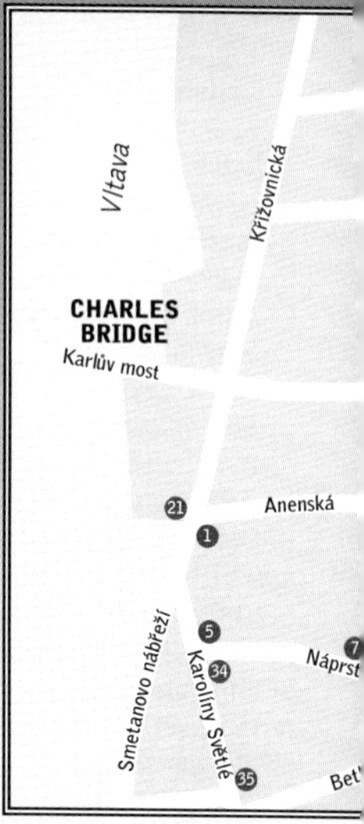

Map labels: Vltava, Křižovnická, CHARLES BRIDGE, Karlův most, Anenská, Smetanovo nábřeží, Karoliny Světlé, Náprst, Bet'

KARLOVA
Restaurants

Bellevue ❶

Smetanovo nábřeží 18

✆ 2222 1438

🚊 Trams 17 and 18

Open: Mon–Sat 1200–1500, 1730–2300

Reservations recommended

All credit cards accepted

International

❸❸❸

This superior French restaurant on the Smetana Embankment enjoys wonderful views of Prague Castle. Dinner for two will set you back a bit but you may feel it's worth it, once you've savoured nouvelle cuisine cooking which meets the highest standards. Live jazz and champagne are served up with Sunday brunch.

Flambée ❷

Betlem Palais, Husova 5

✆ 2424 8512

Ⓜ Metro Staroměstská

Open: daily 1130–0100

Reservations essential

All credit cards accepted

French

❸❸❸

This exclusive restaurant boasts an award-winning chef, an historic setting – the 14th-century cellar is built on Romanesque foundations – and a glitzy clientele (celebrity diners have included Michael Jackson, Tom Cruise and Meryl Streep). Lovers of fresh seafood, oysters especially, will not go away disappointed. Other specialities are venison and Argentine steak. If you haven't had time to book ahead, there's a

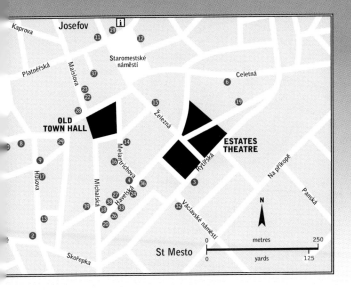

café-bistro on the ground floor.

U Modré Růže ❸

Rytířská 16

✆ 261 081

Ⓜ Metro Můstek

Open: Mon–Sat 1130–2330, Sun 0600–1130

Reservations essential

All credit cards accepted

Czech-International

❸❸❸

'At the Blue Rose' occupies a 15th-century cellar in the heart of the Old Town. The menu is unashamedly exotic, with turtle soup, conger eel, ostrich, alligator and rattlesnake to the fore, or you may prefer the less showy items – baked sole, for example, or aubergine Provençal with Czech Hermelín cheese. The apple bake with cranberries rounds off the meal nicely. The live piano music can be a bit intrusive at times.

▲ Norwegian salmon

Mucha ❹

Melantrichova 5

✆ 263 586

🚇 Metro Staroměstská

Open: daily 1200–1600, 1800–2400

Reservations recommended

All credit cards accepted

Czech

●● ●●●

Named after the famous master of art nouveau, Alfons Mucha, this elegant salon features an eye-catching glass ceiling. The cooking is Czech-inspired, with hints of nouvelle cuisine here and there. If you have a sweet tooth, try the roast breast of duck served with honey and fried bananas. Heartier traditional dishes include goulash Prague-style (in a beer sauce) and roast leg of pork. Music, in palm-court vein, helps to make for a relaxing evening.

Opera Grill ❺

Karolíny Světlé 35

✆ 0602 203962

🚇 Trams 17 and 18

Open: daily 1800–0200

Reservations essential

All credit cards accepted

Czech-International

●●●

If the clientele is anything to go by (Nicole Kidman, Gary Oldman et al), Opera Grill is definitely in vogue. It's also perfectly located for pre-theatre dinners (the Rudolfinum, the Estates Theatre and the National are all within striking distance). Typical dishes include boneless roast duck, and venison with berry sauce, and there are French as well as local wines to choose from. The plush décor with cake-icing finish may be a bit over-the-top for some tastes.

U Pavouka ❻

Celetná 17

✆ 231 3327

🚇 Metro Náměstí Republiky

Open: daily 1130–1500, 1700–2400; snack bar and terrace 1000–2200

Reservations recommended

All credit cards accepted

Czech

●●

'At the Spider' has been around since Communist times and still appears to be holding its own. Celetná, once a street specialising in bakeries, was an important stage on the Royal Route – U Pavouka dates from 1700. The plain Czech cooking – beef stroganoff, pork and chips, pancakes with jam and whipped cream – is acceptable if nothing special. The set menus are good value: chicken bouillon, followed by quarter of duck, red cabbage and dumplings with apple strudel and whipped cream to follow, all at a snip.

Le Petit Chablis ❼

Náprstkova 8

✆ 2222 1019

🚇 Trams 17 and 18

Open: Mon–Sat 1100–1400, 1900–2400

Reservations essential

All credit cards accepted

French

●●●

A quality French restaurant with attentive service and a warm, seductive ambience serves typical dishes include *foie gras*, frogs' legs and venison cooked with pear. Try to save room for one of the homemade desserts. Live music.

Reykjavík ❽

Karlova 20

✆ 2222 1218

🚇 Metro Staroměstská

Open: daily 1100–2400

Reservations recommended

All credit cards accepted

International

€€

As the name implies, this luminary on the culinary scene is an offshoot of the Icelandic Embassy. Fish, naturally enough, is the speciality, flown in fresh from Scandinavia every day and, if you bear this in mind, the prices appear very reasonable. Affable staff and an atmosphere conducive to relaxed conversation.

U Svatého Huberta ❾

Husova 7

✆ 2222 1706

Ⓜ Metro Staroměstská

Open: daily 1130–1600, 1730–2300

Reservations recommended

🚈 🚈

Czech

€€

Game is the speciality here, signalled by the antlers on the white-washed cellar walls and the animal skins covering the wooden seats. The atmosphere is intimate – just a couple of smallish rooms. Typical dishes include breast of pheasant au gratin with mushrooms, and fallow deer with cream sauce. There's a choice of local wines, or, if you prefer, Krušovice beer available on draught.

V Zátíší ❿

Liliová 1

✆ 2222 1155

Ⓜ Metro Staroměstská

Open: daily 1200–1500, 1730–2300

Reservations recommended

All credit cards accepted

Czech-International

€€€

Egon Ronay awarded V Zátíší (the name means 'Still Life') the title 'Eastern European Restaurant of the Year' and it remains one of Prague's most highly prized centres of culinary excellence. You're unlikely to be disappointed with anything here, but the langoustines deserve special mention. Conveniently located near Bethlehem Square.

▲ Roast duck at V Zátíší

KARLOVA
Bars, cafés and pubs

Café Milena ⑪

Staroměstské náměstí 22

☏ 260 843

🚇 Metro Náměstí Republiky

Open: daily 1000–2100

€

You'll find this cosy café on the first floor of the Franz Kafka centre on Old Town Square – there's a small exhibition on the writer in the foyer. Light meals include an appetising choice of salads, all accompanied by a live pianist.

Café Puškin ⑬

Husova 14

☏ 232 1236

🚇 Metro Staroměstská

Open: daily 1200–2400

€€–€€€

Short on atmosphere, but handily situated in the house 'At the Golden Apple', Café Puškin has *borshcht* (beetroot soup) on the lunchtime menu – the only connection with the Russian writer.

Café Rincón ⑭

Melantrichova 12

☏ 266 498

🚇 Metro Můstek

Open: daily 1000–2400

€€

Large, noisy eatery which proves popular with foreign visitors. As the name implies, the food is Mexican-inspired – gazpacho, tortillas, enchiladas, *calamares* and salads. There's a restaurant on the first floor.

Caffreys ⑫

Staroměstské náměstí 10

☏ 2482 8031

🚇 Metro Náměstí Republiky

Open: daily 0900–0100 (Fri–Sat until 0200)

€€

Irish pub where the dishes have a genuine Celtic flavour, for example beef and oyster pie with Guinness, Old Dublin coddle (Irish sausages, bacon, potatoes and onions), Irish lamb stew, and wild salmon with sorrel. A useful stopover if you've missed breakfast in the hotel, Caffreys also turns out doorstep sandwiches.

Chelsea's Bar ⑮

Železná 25

☏ 2161 0234

🚇 Metro Můstek

Open: daily 1100–2400

€€

Akin to an English pub in atmosphere, the bar's strengths are draught beers –Murphys, Celt, Velvet and Staropramen – and filling lunchtime dishes (including pastas, *fajitas* and pancakes). The music is equally eclectic with DJs performing from 2100 at weekends.

Country Life ⑯

Melantrichova 15/Michalská 18

☏ 2421 3366

🚇 Metro Můstek

▲ Cafés on Old Town Square

Open: Mon–Thu 0900–2030,
Fri 0900–1430, Sun 1100–
1700

₵

Large, self-service
restaurant sharing
premises with the health
food shop of the same
name. All items on the
menu are strictly vege-
tarian, using only plant-
based ingredients.

Ethno ⑰

Husova 10

∅ 232 7940

🚇 Metro Staroměstská

Open: Sun–Thu 1000–2300,
Fri–Sat 1000–2400

₵

The ethnic bric-à-brac,
ranging from African
cane fans and exotic
fabric parrots to
Guatemalan woodcarv-
ings, all contributes to
the cheerful atmosphere
in this lively, modern
café. Coffee, cocktails
and tiramisu.

Havelská Koruna ⑱

Havelská 23

∅ 2423 5574

🚇 Metro Můstek

Open: daily 0930–1700

₵₵

A self-service restaurant
in a 14th-century house.
You pick up a card on
entering, choose from
the wide range of meat,
fish and vegetarian
dishes on offer and pay
as you leave.

Hop Store ⑲

Ovocný trh

∅ 2423 4794

▲ Klub Lavka

🚇 Metro Náměstí Republiky

Open: daily 1000–2400

₵

You'll find this new,
ultra-hip microbrewery
opposite the Estates
Theatre. The highly
palatable home brew
goes down a treat; alter-
natively, there's a huge
array of bottled beers
on offer, as well as
salads and sandwiches.

In vino veritas ⑳

Havelská 12

∅ 267 476

🚇 Metro Můstek

Open: daily 1000–2400

₵₵

Friendly Italian trattoria
doing a brisk business
in pasta dishes, polenta
and pancakes. Equally
tempting is the 'big
salad', a motley dish of
egg, pepper, cheese,
carrot, lettuce, tomato,
cucumber and sweet
corn. Weather permit-
ting, you can sit at a
table on the pavement.

Klub Lavka ㉑

Novotného lavka 1

∅ 2421 4797

🚋 Trams 17 and 18

Open: daily 0900–0100

₵₵

This vast entertainment
complex occupies a
prime spot overlooking
the River Vltava –
there's a riverside
terrace and cocktail bar
(tequilas are a
speciality). Other attractions include indoor and
outdoor dining spaces, a
theatre, a dance floor
and an internet café.

U Minuty ㉒

Staroměstské náměstí 2

∅ None available

🚇 Metro Náměstí Republiky

Open: Mon–Sat 1000–2300

₵₵

'At the Minute', an his-
toric house on Old Town
Square, is where the
writer Franz Kafka lived
from 1889–96. It's now
re-opened as a café with
a no-smoking policy. As

well as the advertised 60 varieties of tea and 40 different servings of coffee, there's Czech beer and 'Eucharistical wines from the archbishop's vaults'!

U Mravence

U Radnice 20	
∅ None available	
Ⓜ Metro Staroměstská	
Open: daily 1100–2400	

The café-bar 'At the Ants' sells memorably scrumptious snacks – toasted sandwiches, chips with salsa, quiches, filled rolls (such as spinach with cream cheese), brownies, muffins and cheesecake. There's a good selection of wines.

Praha Tamura ㉔

Havelská 6	
∅ 2423 2056	
Ⓜ Metro Můstek	
Open: daily 1100–2300	
ⓔⓒ	

Tiny Japanese food shop and buffet restaurant near Havelská market with a tempting selection of fish and vegetable *sashimi*, sushi and *tempura*. If you're not sure what to choose, the fixed price menu is good value.

Roma Due ㉕

Liliová 18	
∅ 0606 287 943	
Ⓜ Metro Staroměstská	
Open: daily 1030–2400	
ⓔⓒ	

A roomy pizzeria in a convenient central location, with a wood-fired oven and friendly waiters. There's another branch **Roma Uno** (*Jagellonská 16*).

Safir Grill ㉖

Havelská 12	
∅ None available	
Ⓜ Metro Můstek	
Open: Mon–Sat 1000–2000	
ⓔ	

Useful fast food counter, doing a brisk trade in *falafel*, kebabs, houmous, yoghurts and other Middle-Eastern fare.

Staropražský Klub ㉗

Havelská 7	
∅ None available	
Ⓜ Metro Můstek	
Open: daily 0800–2200	
ⓔ	

This busy market café with quirky décor, including a purloined station clock and an art-nouveau stair rail, serves hearty breakfasts as well as cakes and pastries.

TGI Friday's ㉘

Malé náměstí 2	
∅ 2422 1230	
Ⓜ Metro Staroměstská	
Open: Mon–Thu 1200–1400, Fri 1200–1500, Sat 1000–1500, Sun 1000–1400	
ⓔ	

A branch of the well-known American chain whose strengths include friendly service, an upbeat atmosphere, inventive cocktails and excellent snacks, from Caesar salad and potato skins to burgers and ribs.

Vivaldi ㉙

Karlova 46	
∅ None available	
Ⓜ Metro Staroměstská	
Open: daily 1000–2400; beer bar 1100–0200	
ⓔⓒ–ⓔⓒⓒ	

There's a choice of 15 pizzas as well as pasta dishes and omelettes. Downstairs is the pub U Karla IV, dispensing Pilsner Urquell, Gambrinus (light and dark), Murphys and many other beers.

U Zlatého Hada ㉚

Karlova 18	
∅ 2222 2160	
Ⓜ Metro Staroměstská	
Open: daily 1000–2400	
ⓔⓒ	

Always busy, this labyrinthine hostelry is only a stone's throw from the Charles Bridge. The menu is eclectic to say the least – fillet of salmon in Tokay (Hungarian) wine with saffron rice, or braised Prague ham with dumplings and sauerkraut, and Swiss cheese fondue.

KARLOVA
Shops, markets and picnic sites

Čajovna **31**

Betlémské náměstí 1

🔵 Metro Staroměstská

Open: daily 1000–1900

This former beer bar near the Bethlehem Chapel has now switched to teas: green monkey, gunpowder, jasmine, Earl Grey, China and Darjeeling to name but a few.

Country Life **16**

Melantrichova 15

🔵 Metro Můstek

Open: Mon–Thu 0900–2030, Fri 0900–1600, Sun 1100–2030

Now well established, this health food store is in great demand. Products include veggie sandwiches, freshly baked whole wheat bread, dried fruit, muesli, grains, beans and soya products.

E Kliment **32**

Na Mustku 8

🔵 Metro Můstek

Open: Mon–Fri 0730–1900, Sat 0800–1800, Sun 0900–1800

A traditional Czech *lahůdky* (delicatessen) offering a predictable range of cooked meats as well as bread, coffee and other groceries.

Market Mix **33**

Havelská 4

🔵 Metro Můstek

Open: Mon–Fri 0800–1900, Sat 0800–1230

Grocery store with a takeaway counter offering snacks, coffee, tea and alcohol.

Pekařství **34**

Náprstkova 7

🔵 Trams 17 and 18

Open: Mon–Sat 0800–2000, Sun 0900–2000

A little off the beaten track, this new bakery with café sells freshly filled baguettes.

Pekařství **35**

Karoliny Svetlé 23

🔵 Trams 17 and 18

Open: Mon–Fri 0700–1900, Sat 0800–1600

Useful bakery with a small takeaway counter (pizzas, pastries, salads and *zakuski*).

Tomaš Kolouch **36**

Havelská 9

🔵 Metro Můstek

Open: Mon–Fri 0800–1700

▲ Havelská Market

Follow the passageway beneath the emblem of the rearing horse and you'll come to this large supermarket, with deli and drinks counter for coffees and snacks.

Uzeniny **37**

U Radnice 2

🔵 Metro Staroměstská

Open: Mon–Fri 0830–1700

Tucked away in an arcade, next door to the **U Radnice** restaurant, this small butcher's shop with deli counter specialises in Moravian produce.

U Zlaté Váhy **38**

Havelská 3

🔵 Metro Můstek

Open: Mon–Fri 0700–1800, Sat 0700–1200

'At the Scales' is a convenience store near the market trading in dairy and meat products with a deli counter.

Havelské tržiště **39**

Havelská

🔵 Metro Můstek

Open: Mon–Sat 0700–1800, Sun 0830–1730

Handy for the Old Town sights, this large fruit and vegetable market also deals in souvenirs.

U Kalicha (The Flagon)

The Good Soldier Švejk

It's one of the most famous moments in Czech literature. Josef Švejk, a bumbling corporal in the Austrian army, is about to take leave of a friend en route to the front. As they part he calls out, 'When the war's over, look me up. You'll find me in The Flagon every evening at six o'clock'. To which the friend replies, 'Right you are. After the war, at six o'clock'. When author Josef Hašek died in 1923, aged only 38, he left more than 500 essays, sketches, poems and articles behind him, but the satirical masterpiece he had been working on for years remained incomplete. *The Good Soldier Švejk* was published posthumously in 1930.

Švejk, a warm-hearted, simple-minded 'man of the people', is always getting into scrapes with authority but somehow it's authority that comes off second best. His adventures begin immediately after the assassination of the Archduke Franz Ferdinand at Sarajevo. Turning up for his usual pint in The Flagon, Švejk is overheard speaking disrespectfully about the monarchy by Bretschneider, a member of the secret police, and arrested, along with the landlord. Drafted into the army, he is suspected of malingering before being certified 'feeble-minded'. In recounting Švejk's subsequent exploits across the length and breadth of the Empire, Hašek satirises the cruelties and absurdities of army life, the bureaucratic incompetence typical of the Austro-Hungarian Empire in its death throes, the Roman Catholic Church and, most unsparingly, war itself.

The cast of comic characters includes Švejk's charwoman Mrs Müller, the publican's wife Mrs Palivec, the bullying Sergeant-Major Repa, the military chaplain Otto Katz, whose favourite tipple is communion wine, the hapless ladies' man Lieutenant Lukáš, and the appropriately named Baloun, who manages to get through the best part of the regimental rations single-handed.

Hašek introduces more than a little of himself into his comic masterpiece. Like his hero, he sold dogs of dubious pedigree to unsuspecting owners, frequented Prague's pubs, including U Kalicha, served in the Austrian army during World War I and became a Russian prisoner of war. The illustrations for Švejk

were drawn by an old friend, Josef Lada, and are as memorable and well-loved as the book itself.

U Kalicha is geared exclusively to tourists (the menu is published in 16 languages, including Japanese) and trades mercilessly on its literary associations. Many of the Czech dishes recall characters from the book, Lada's illustrations appear on napkins and beer mats, the staff wear period costumes and an old-fashioned brass band entertains the customers, who need little encouragement to buy the Švejk-inspired souvenirs from the pub shop. Be prepared to sit elbow-to-elbow with fellow diners and don't expect too much from the food – you come for the atmosphere. Unless your appetite is gargantuan, avoid the 'eat all you can' menu – the price isn't worth the damage you can do to your stomach.

There are three dining areas:
• **Café Klara** Open: daily 0800–1600. This attractive bar, with polished wooden tables, pub mirrors and stained-glass doors, serves hot meals from 1000 until 1400, including goulash with dumplings, pork with cream, and beef with Mrs Müller's mushroom sauce.
• **Beer Bar** Open: daily 1000–2400. This tiny 'spit-and-sawdust' bar, decorated with sepia photographs of Old Prague, serves similar fare to the restaurant but at reduced prices. It's a tradition for visitors to add graffiti to the walls.

▲ Hostinec U Kalicha

• **Hostinec U Kalicha (The Flagon Restaurant)** (∅ 290 701; open: daily 1100–2200; live music from 1930; reservations essential (a couple of days in advance during the summer); all credit cards accepted; Czech; ❶❷ – ❶❷❸) The main beer hall seats 200. The walls are decorated with Švejk-inspired cartoons and visitors' signatures.

Recommended Švejk menu selections are: Widow Palivec's chicken salad, roulade à la Feldkurat [Otto] Katz, goulash à la Kalich, Bretschneider's bowl for two, beefsteak à la Lieutenant Lukáš, Baloun's baking tin. Other specialities include potato pancakes, goose liver, goats' cheese, roasted piglet and roast trout. All meals are served with dumplings, sauerkraut and potatoes or chips. Desserts include apple strudel with almonds and whipped cream, fruit dumplings and Kaiser Palatschinken (sweet pancakes).

Souvenirs on sale in the shop include Švejk glasses, tankards, dolls, T-shirts, tablecloths, matches, badges, key rings, pencils and ash trays, among other things.

> 'When the war's over, look me up. You'll find me in The Flagon every evening at six o'clock.'

Národní Třída

The backstreets of this area, largely undiscovered by tourists, are full of bars and cheap, neighbourhood restaurants. The main thoroughfare, Národní, is the address of two of Prague's best known cafés, the Slavia and Café Louvre.

NÁRODNÍ TŘÍDA
Restaurants

U Bubeníčků ❶

Myslikova 8

✆ 295 641

🚇 Metro Karlovo náměstí

Open: daily 1100–2300

Reservations unnecessary

Czech

€€

'The Little Drummer Girl' is a lively, informal *vinárna* with attractive wooden décor, serving traditional Czech dishes including beefsteak with eggs, pork ribs and potato pancakes. Both Gambrinus and Krušovice dark beer are available on draught, while the live music ranges from jazz to country and folk with occasional disco evenings.

Buenos Aires ❷

Křemencová 7

✆ 2491 3183

🚇 Metro Národní Třída

Open: daily 1100–2300

Reservations recommended

All credit cards accepted

Argentinian

€€€

In a country where beef is plentiful and appreciated, the current fad for pampas-reared Argentine steaks is hardly surprising. Start perhaps with *chorizo* (tangy sausage served with *chimichuri* sauce, then follow with your choice of cut (price is by weight, 150–250g). Children can order from a small kids' menu. There's a bright, lively feel to the place, especially on Fridays when it's generally live music night.

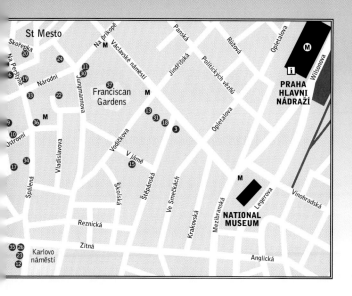

Česky-Americky Restaurant ❸

Štěpánská 63

Ⓒ 2421 6935

Ⓜ Metro Můstek

Open: daily 1100–2300

Reservations unnecessary

All credit cards accepted

Czech-American

Ⓒ Ⓒ

Just around the corner from Wenceslas Square, this hospitable eatery is much patronised by shoppers and local businessmen. There are two rooms – an elegant salon on the first floor and a brash American outfit downstairs with stars-and-stripes décor and garish, graffiti-style friezes on the walls.

The highlight of the Czech menu is St Wenceslas Spear (leg of pork with chicken breast and bacon).

Dynamo ❹

Pštrossova 29

Ⓒ 294 224

Ⓒ Trams 6, 9, 18, 21 and 22

Open: daily 1000–2400

Reservations unnecessary

💳💳 American Express

International

Ⓒ Ⓒ

Tucked away in a backstreet near the National Theatre, Dynamo has yet to establish itself on the restaurant scene. Plain modern furnishings set the tone of friendly informality. The lunch menu is simple but appealing: spicy chicken, fried fish, potato wedges, spinach tagliatelle. The à la carte menu offers the usual mixture of steaks and roasts.

Gargoyles ❺

Opatovická 5

Ⓒ 2491 6047

Ⓒ Trams 6, 9, 18, 21 and 22

Open: daily 1100–1500, 1700–2400

Reservations recommended

All credit cards accepted

International

Ⓒ Ⓒ Ⓒ

In this establishment, run by an ambitious

Restaurant

DYNAMO

Pštrossova 220/29_Praha 1_T 29 42 24

young Californian, whose enthusiasm is infectious, the watchwords are informality and experiment. The chef is adventurous in his approach, willing to take risks, even if they don't always come off. You can eat à la carte if you wish, but the 'Chef's choice' – a five-course surprise – will introduce you to the best of what's on offer. Starters include a succulent braised duck salad with goats' cheese, saffron and pearl onions, while two of the main courses, halibut with couscous and spinach salad, and grilled pork chop with roasted pear and potato fennel au gratin, deserve specially high marks.

U Medvídků ❻

Na Perštýné 7

✆ 2421 1916

🚇 Metro Národní Třída

Open: Mon–Fri 1600–0300, Sat 1800–0300, Sun 1800–0100; restaurant Mon–Sat 1130–2300, Sun 1130–2200

Reservations recommended

All credit cards accepted

Czech

❷❸

'At the Little Bear' is one of Prague's oldest beer halls. Founded in 1466, it was rebuilt in the 19th century with a glass roof – the courtyard is also under cover. The pub-restaurant caters mainly for tourists, especially in the evenings. There's an English language menu but no set meals – everything is à la carte. The food is in the lusty Bohemian tradition. You can order snacks, if you're not partial to pickled herring or liverwurst with onions. Draught Budvar is served throughout the day while there's musical entertainment in the form of a brass band or accordion ensemble. This place is best enjoyed in the company of friends so you can have a laugh and a knees-up!

Parnas ❼

Smetanovo nábřeží 2

✆ 2421 1901

🚋 Trams 17 and 18

Open: daily 1130–1500, 1800–2400

Reservations recommended

All credit cards accepted

International

❷❸–❹❺❻

One of Prague's few gourmet temples, Parnas is also a 'room with a view', with vistas embracing the Charles Bridge, Prague Castle and the orchards and gardens of the Lesser Town. The art-nouveau décor creates an appropriate environment for the fabulous food, served by piano accompaniment.

Pohoda ❽

Masarykovo nábřeží 2

✆ 298 628

🚋 Trams 17 and 21

Open: daily 1130–2200

Reservations recommended

No credit cards accepted

International

❷❸

The name suggests cosiness and the ochre-painted exterior is calculated to draw you in from this bleak stretch of the Masaryk

Embankment. Inside it's smart and comfortable, though the atmosphere can be a little low key. And while the food can't match the standard of some of the classier restaurants in the neighbourhood, the prices are a lot more realistic.

Rôtisserie 9

Mikulandská 6

✆ 2491 4557

🚊 Trams 6, 9, 18, 21 and 22

Open: Mon–Sat 1130–1530, 1730–2330, Sun 1730–2330

Reservations unnecessary

No credit cards accepted

Czech

❶–❷❷

A touch too formal perhaps, but the food in this quaint dining room is excellent value, whether you opt for the fixed price menu or eat à la carte. The menu (available in English) offers few surprises apart from Danish caviar. If you're really hungry, throw caution to the winds and settle down to a Bohemian platter of roast pork, with ham, duck, dumplings, potato pancakes and red and white sauerkraut. Alternatively, try one of the chef's special flambéed dishes.

Thanh Long 10

Ostrovní 23

✆ 2491 2318

🚇 Metro Národní Třída

Open: daily 1130–1500, 1700–2330

Reservations recommended

All credit cards accepted

Thai

❷❷

While Prague isn't exactly renowned for its Thai food, Thanh Long goes some way to making up the deficit. Not that it helps its own cause by advertising 150 Chinese and Asian specials, a boast which can only confuse. Moravian and German wines are available, although you may find a chilled bottle of Budvar preferable. It can be very busy, especially at weekends.

NÁRODNÍ TŘÍDA
Bars, cafés and pubs

Bistro Sights

Jungmannovo náměstí 7

⌀ 0602 381734

Ⓜ Metro Můstek

Open: daily 0900–2000

●●

The distracting window décor includes huge cacti, fishing nets and other bric-à-brac. Appetising 'sweet honey' breakfasts of fruit pancakes are served from 0830 to 1100 daily. Snacks include omelettes, sand-wiches and croissants while the lunch menu (roast duck, chicken and chips, homemade apple pie) is excellent value.

Bufet Cukrárna ⑫

Karlovo náměští 20

⌀ None available

Ⓣ Trams 3, 6, 14, 18, 21, 22 and 24

Open: Mon–Fri 0830–2000, Sat–Sun 0900–2030

●

Self-service café with a bright, cheerful ambi-ence. Snack menu includes soups, chicken pieces and pastries to eat in or takeaway.

Buffalo Bill's ⑬

Vodičkova 9

⌀ 2494 8624

Ⓣ Trams 3, 9, 14 and 24

Open: daily 1200–2400

All credit cards accepted

●●–●●●

Lively, popular Tex-Mex bar and grill, offering succulent ribs, wings, burritos, tacos and heaped salads.

Café Louvre ㊳

Národní 20

⌀ 297 223/2491 2230

Ⓣ Trams 6, 9, 18, 21 and 22

Open: daily 1000–2400

●●

Restored to its former glory in the early 1990s, this celebrated first floor café looks out on to one of Prague's most splendid avenues. Unusually for this city, there's a non-smoking room, as well as billiard tables and international newspapers. As for the food, Café Louvre is well known for its breakfasts but there's also a choice of appetising hot dishes throughout the day.

Globe Bookshop and Café ⑭

Pštrossova 6

⌀ 2491 7230

Ⓣ Trams 6, 9, 18, 21 and 22

Open: Mon–Thu 0800–2400, Fri 0800–0100, Sat 1000–0100, Sun 1000–2400

●

Following recent trends, this friendly bookshop, formerly in Holešovice, has internet access and a large café at the rear. Choose between muffins, brownies, cookies, takeaway coffees, hash browns, eggs and omelettes, cereals, muesli, crois-sants, soups, pâté, salads, sandwiches … the list goes on.

Jáma ⑮

V jámě 7

⌀ 9000 0312

Ⓣ Trams 3, 9, 14, 21 and 24

Open: Mon–Fri 1100–0100, Sat–Sun 1300–0100

●●

'The Pit' but definitely not 'the pits'! This bois-terous American bar offers beer in abun-dance, good conversa-tion and a wide-ranging menu.

Káva-Káva-Káva ⑯

Národní 37

⌀ 268 409

Ⓣ Trams 6, 9, 18, 21 and 22

Open: Mon–Fri 0700–2000, Sat–Sun 0900–2000

●

This small café-bar has internet access and a non-smoking section downstairs. The entrance is through a courtyard (look for the lions on the gates). Try the freshly roasted whole-bean coffee.

Kavárna Velryba

Opatovická 24

∅ 2491 2391

Ⓜ Metro Národní Třída

Open: daily 1100–0200

Ⓔ

The 'Whale Café' opened in 1992 and became such a hit with Prague's students and artists that a gallery soon opened in the sitting room next door. This convivial dive with its trademark faded wallpaper, Spartan furnishings and subterranean bar mostly deals in bottles of Gambrinus, although there's also a good selection of whiskies. Food is mainly restricted to snacks – the dish of the day is served with a generous helping of chips.

Lucerna Café ⑱

Palác Lucerna shopping precinct, Vodičkova – Stepanská

∅ None available

Ⓜ Metro Muzeum

Open: daily 1000–2400

Ⓔ–ⒺⒺ

The café and piano bar on the first floor of the passage dates from the First World War and has a certain period charm.

Na Perštýné ⑲

Na Perštýné 8

∅ 265 625

Ⓜ Trams 6, 9, 18, 21 and 22

Open: daily 1100–2300

Ⓔ–ⒺⒺ

In this bright, modern snack bar with a friendly, relaxed atmosphere the Pilsner Urquell on draught is a sound enough reason to visit if you're a beer lover, while vegetarians will appreciate the cheese and mushroom risotto – most of the other dishes are in the meaty mainstream.

Restaurant Jarmark ⑱

Palác Lucerna shopping precinct, Vodičkova – Stepanská

∅ 2423 3733

Ⓜ Metro Muzeum

Open: Mon–Fri 0800–2200, Sat–Sun 1100–2200

ⒺⒺ

Genteel, amazingly cheap, self-service restaurant, offering an assortment of salads, grills, stir-fries, pastries and fresh fruit. No one leaves hungry!

Skořepka ⑳

Skořepka 1

∅ 2421 4715

Ⓜ Metro Můstek

Open: daily 1100–0100

Ⓔ

Potential customers are initially attracted by the décor – you can hardly miss the cart suspended rather improbably from the ceiling. Krušovice lager is available, as well as coffee, both at ground level and in the upstairs gallery.

Slavia Kavárna ㉑

Smetanovo nábřeží/Národní 2

∅ 2422 0957

Ⓜ Trams 6, 9, 18, 21 and 22

Open: Mon–Fri 0800–2400, Sat–Sun 0900–2400

ⒺⒺ

An institution almost from the moment it opened in 1863, the Slavia's previous patrons included the writer, Franz Kafka. Today's regulars cover a broad spectrum of Prague society, from old ladies pampering their pet dogs to bohemian types, mainly actors from the National Theatre across the street. Grab a window table if you can – there are great views across the River Vltava towards Prague Castle. Meals include fishermen's soup and beef sirloin marinated in armagnac, served with mushrooms, leeks and wild rice – delicious!

NÁRODNÍ TŘÍDA
Shops, markets and picnic sites

Cukrárna Monika 🅽
Charvátova 11
🅼 Metro Národní Třída
Open: Mon–Fri 0900–1900,
Sat 1000–1900, Sun 1100–
1800

Small city-centre bakery offering a wide selection of confectionery and ice creams.

Leonidas 🅽
Karlovo náměstí 17
🅽 Trams 3, 6, 14, 18, 21, 22 and 24
Open: Mon–Fri 1000–1800

Cukrárna selling sweets, Belgian pralines and novelty chocolates.

Musetti 🅽
Perlová 8
🅼 Metro Můstek
Open: daily 0900–2000

An appealing Italian *cukrárna*, offering a range of desserts and ice creams. Popular with all ages.

Jan Paukert 🅽
Národní 20
🅽 Trams 6, 9, 18, 21 and 22
Open: Mon–Fri 0800–1900, Sat 0900–1400

This gourmet delicatessen in a renovated old building is a prize find. Besides an excellent selection of meat cuts, salads and imported cheeses, you'll find alcoholic drinks including Bohemia Sekt, and a choice of Czech wines including Cabernet Sauvignon from Mikulka. There is a restaurant upstairs.

Lahůdky 🅽
Karlovo náměstí 8
🅽 Trams 3, 6, 14, 18, 21, 22 and 24
Open: Mon–Fri 0630–1830, Sat 0800–1200

There's a large meat and cheese counter and also bread and drinks.

Maso-Uzeniny 🅽
Na Perštýně 9
🅼 Metro Národní Třída
Open: Mon–Fri 0800–1800, Sat 0830–1500

This traditional butcher's shop with a snack bar and rotisserie also sells cheese, beer and other alcoholic drinks.

Mini-market 🅽
Karoliny Svetlé 3
🅽 Trams 17 and 18
Open: Mon–Sat 0800–2300, Sun 0800–2100

This is a useful mini-market near the National Theatre.

Nápoje 🅽
Křemencová 7
🅼 Metro Národní Třída
Open: Mon–Fri 0700–1900, Sat 0900–1300

Grocery shop with a good supply of alcoholic drinks, including Czech sparkling wine.

Na Zlatém Kříži 🅽
Jungmannovo náměstí 19
🅼 Metro Můstek
Open: Mon–Fri 0730–1800, Sat 0900–1800

A delicatessen selling a good selection of open sandwiches and salad snacks. There's also a drinks counter touting beers, wines, spirits and liqueurs, including Becherovka.

Pasaž Lucerna 🅽
Off Wenceslas Square
🅽 Trams 3, 9, 14 and 24
Open: Mon–Sun 1000–2100

Stepanská entrance
Cellarius: Wines from round the world including French champagnes and quality Czech wines, including Modre Portugal. The branch at Budečská 29 has a wooden terrace for tastings.

Vodičkova entrance
There's a confectioner's with bakery opposite the Jarmark restaurant. Next door is a delicatessen

which also sells alcoholic and soft drinks.

Potraviny ㉜

Pštrossova, corner of Na struze

🚊 Trams 6, 9, 18, 21 and 22

Open: Mon–Fri 0800–1900, Sat 0830–1800

Grocery store with a fruit and vegetable stall next door.

Tesco ㉝

Národní 26

🚇 Metro Národní Třída

Open: Mon–Fri 0700–2000, Sat 0800–1900, Sun 0900–1900

At this Czech branch of the British chain, the supermarket is on the lower ground floor. For a small fee, Tesco will deliver to any destination in central Prague between 1400 and 2000 (for orders purchased before 1300). There's a small café by the entrance selling sandwiches, filled rolls, pizzas, pastries and salads to take away.

Uzenářství a pekařství ㉞

Spálená 47

🚊 Tram 17

Open: Mon–Fri 0900–1900, Sat 0830–1300

Bakery-cum-butchers with deli counter displays of sausages and smoked meats. The bread shop next door also sells pizza slices, rolls, apple turnovers and other scrummy pastries.

V Slavska Pasaž ㉟

Karlovo náměstí 6

🚊 Trams 3, 6, 14, 18, 21, 22 and 24

Open: Mon–Fri 0900–1900, Sat 1000–1900, Sun 1100–1900; pizzeria 0930–2200

A small shopping precinct off Charles Square with a *cukrárna* (cakes and pastries shop). There are tables set out under the glass roof of the passage with palms and umbrellas for decoration. So sit back and relax!

Markets

Národní Třída ㊱

🚇 Metro Národní Třída

Open: daily 0900–1900

Just outside the metro station there's a small, but useful, fruit and vegetable market.

Picnic sites

Franciscan Gardens ㊲

🚇 Metro Můstek

Tucked away behind Wenceslas Square, the Franciscan Gardens takes its name from the adjoining medieval church, which was never completed. Popular with Prague office workers, the benches are laid out around a formal trellis garden.

▲ Franciscan Gardens

Czech beer

The golden nectar

The Czechs' love affair with the golden nectar began in the days of King Wenceslas and has never faded – Czech drinkers still hold the world record for beer consumption per capita – 279 litres! It was during the 14th century that Charles IV of Bohemia first saw the commercial possibilities, encouraging the trade to flourish in Prague's 36 breweries, while outlawing the export of hops. Rudolf II took an equally keen interest: in 1583 he acquired the **Krušovice** brewery, renowned for its highly-prized **Zatec** hops, and honoured it with the royal patent – you can see his portrait on pub signs and beer mats even today.

▲ Pilsner Urquell

Brewing was also big business in the southern Bohemian town of České Budějovice – Budweis to give it its German name. The American beer, Budweiser, has nothing in common with the heavy, semi-sweet Czech version, currently known as **Budweiser Budvar**. The trademark remains a bone of contention: for the best part of a century, the American brewers, Anheuser Busch have been trying to buy into the state-owned Czech company, to date without success.

Most of today's beers are pale lagers or Pilsners. In 1842 a consortium of businessmen in the industrial town of Plzeň in western Bohemia, called in a Bavarian master brewer, Josef Groll, to improve the quality of the local ale. He came up with **Pilsner Urquell**, a bottom-fermented beer using Czech malt, flavoursome local hops and exceptionally soft water. For this gift to mankind Groll deserves to go down in history. Aficionados should know that in the Czech Republic Pilsner Urquell is sometimes known as **Plzeňský Prazdroj**. **Gambrinus** comes from the same stable and will appeal to drinkers who prefer something a little smoother and less bitter. The Plzeň brewery sets great store by its new pale brew, **Primus.**

While you're in Prague you should try other well-known pale lagers such as the local

Staropramen, full-bodied and refreshing, and **Kozel** (The Goat), a strong, spicy brew produced in Velké Popovice. If you're a fan of dark beer (the colour is the result of roasting or caramelising the malt), be sure to call in at the historic pubs, **U Fleků** (*see below*) and **U Kalicha** (*see page 26*).

Czech beer is commendably free of chemicals and other impurities and it's almost unheard of to be served with an undernourished pint. According to a 19th-century manual, properly fermented beer should be 'pure and clear with a fine lustre', a milky white head and froth that clings to the surface and walls of the pot or glass. The *cognoscenti* advise pushing a matchstick into the foam – if it stays upright for more than 10 seconds it's good.

One point about bottled beers: the percentage figure on the label refers to the malt content. If you want to know the alcoholic strength of a beer, look to the figure in smaller type, although the two indicators usually go hand-in-hand.

> **Czech drinkers still hold the world record for beer consumption per capita – 279 litres!**

▲ U Fleků

• **U Fleků** *Křemencová 11; ℆ 2491 5118;* Ⓜ *metro Národní Třída; open: Mon–Sat 0900– 2300;* ❷❷. Founded in 1499, this famous pub has now been taken over by tourists. Customers sit cheek by jowl at long black tables and consume the famous black beer. The food (of mediocre quality) is traditional pub grub: homemade liver sausage with vinegar and onion, beer cheese with onion and butter, Prague ham with cucumber, smoked saddle of pork with horseradish and cucumber.

• **U Dvou Koček** *Uhelný trh 10; ℆ none available;* Ⓜ *metro Můstek; open: Mon–Sat 0830– 1500, 1600– 2300, Sun 1100– 1500, 1600– 2300;* ❶. Popular with young Praguers, 'At the Two Cats' consists of a beer bar and dining space with traditional wooden furnishings (pub grub includes soups). The beer is Plzenský Prazdroj and there's occasional live music.

• **U Zlatého Tygra** *Husova 17; ℆ none available;* Ⓜ *metro Staroměstská; open: Mon–Sat 1500–2300;* ❶. Václav Havel took Bill Clinton to 'The Golden Tiger', one of Prague's best-loved pubs, during his official visit in 1994. The plain beer hall is furnished with long wooden benches and is often full to bursting with locals who come here for conversation and steady drinking.

Wenceslas Square

Cafés, bars and restaurants have proliferated in this area and are even thicker on the ground than at first sight. The hotels on Wenceslas Square are worth investigating, as are the shopping precincts known locally as 'passages'.

WENCESLAS SQUARE
Restaurants

Fondue ❶

Slezská 20

✆ 2425 0459

🚋 Trams 10 and 16

Open: Mon–Fri 1000–0100, Sat–Sun 1100–0100

Reservations recommended

All credit cards accepted

Fondue

💰💰

Smart cellar eatery with a choice of fondues, including exotic varieties such as pork in curry and chicken prepared with Chinese herbs. You have a good choice of Czech and Austrian wines, including Zweigelt, Rulandské Modre, Frankovka and Riesling.

El Gaucho ❷

Kenvelo Centre, Václavské náměstí 11

✆ 2162 9410

🚇 Metro Můstek

Open: daily 1100–2300

Reservations recommended

All credit cards accepted

Argentinian

💰💰

This typical shopping precinct restaurant on the first floor of the Kenvelo Centre is geared pretty much exclusively to pleasing aficionados of Argentine beefsteak. From rump to T-bone, each juicy off-cut weighs in at 250g to 1kg and is grilled to perfection by experts. Visit during the happy hour (1600–1800) and you'll be rewarded with a 50 per cent reduction on your main course.

Kojak's ❸

Anny Letenské 16

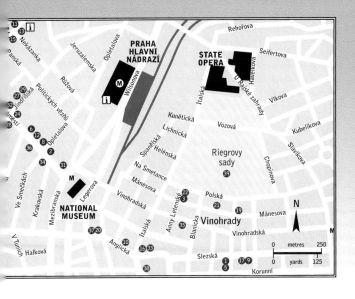

Ø 2225 0594

🚋 Tram 11

Open: Mon–Fri 1130–2400,
Sat–Sun 1500–2400

Reservations recommended

No credit cards accepted

Eclectic

€€

This brash American-
style diner is actually
run by a couple of
Czechs. The food is as
eclectic as the bright,
in-your-face décor – if
in doubt, go for the
Tex-Mex specialities.
The restaurant also
offers a takeaway
delivery service by Food
Taxi (Ø 2251 6732).

Marie Teresie ❹

Na příkopě 23

▲ Europa Hotel

Secession Restaurant ⑥

Europa Hotel, Václavské náměstí 25

✆ 2422 8117

🚊 Trams 3, 9 and 14

Open: daily 1200–1500, 1800–2400

Reservations recommended

All credit cards accepted

Czech

❶❷❸

One of the most wonderful buildings to grace Wenceslas Square, the Europa Hotel was designed in exuberant art-nouveau style in 1903–5. Fans of the movie *Titanic* will be interested to know that the dining room of the doomed liner was modelled on the Secession Restaurant, a sumptuous blend of wood inlay, crystal chandeliers, bronze lamps, carved mirrors and painted glass. The menu might best be described as 'refined Czech': beefsteak with roquefort cheese, lamb cutlets in herb butter and pikeperch *à la meunière*. Breakfast is served from 0700 to 1000 in the art-nouveau café which is also a feast for the eye and a former haunt of the beau monde in the 1920s. Note the antique espresso machine.

✆ 2422 9869

🚇 Metro Můstek

Open: daily 1200–2300

Reservations recommended

All credit cards accepted

Czech

❶❷

Despite the unpromising setting – a phoney cellar in the Rathova passage with a portrait of the famous Empress on the wall – the cooking turns out to be not bad at all, so long as you're partial to traditional Czech fare. Highlights include smoked tongue with horseradish sauce, garlic soup and 'Granny's casserole' – all good value and with an unpretentious atmosphere well suited to a group or party.

Rudý Baron ⑤

Korunní 23

✆ 2251 1348

🚊 Trams 10 and 16

Open: daily 1123–2426

Reservations unnecessary

All credit cards accepted

Czech

❶❷

The décor of this fun restaurant, a quirky shrine to the famed German fighter ace, Manfred von Richthofen (nicknamed the 'Red Baron') includes the suspended wings of a Fokker aircraft, among other First World War memorabilia. Grills and poultry dishes are the culinary mainstays. Children less than 120cm tall can eat free of charge if

Staropražské Rychtě ⑦

Hotel Zlatá Husa, Václavské náměstí 5–7

✆ 2419 3817	
Ⓜ Metro Můstek	
Open: daily 1100–2300	
Reservations recommended	
All credit cards accepted	
Czech	

€€–€€€

A well-known hotel restaurant, fronting Wenceslas Square, which has still not managed to shrug off its rather staid, Communist-era image. That said, the traditional Czech fare: smoked pig's tongue with apple and horseradish, roast beef with tartar sauce, roasted duck with red cabbage and dumplings, is usually up to scratch and there's freshwater fish (carp for example) by way of an alternative – even Malossol caviar if you can afford it.

Teppanyaki Jalta ⑧

Václavské náměstí 45	
✆ 2282 2111	
Ⓜ Metro Muzeum	
Open: daily 1200–1500, 1800–2200	
Reservations essential	
All credit cards accepted	
Japanese	

€€€

Japanese food has not caught on to quite the same degree here as in Vienna but when a major hotel surrenders its kitchen, you know it must be serious. Sushi is served in the lobby bar while beef, vegetable and fish dishes are grilled on the hot-plates of the *teppanyaki* table. *Miso* soup (soya paste

consommé with seaweed and tofu) and yellow-fin tuna count among the highlights of a wide-ranging menu. Traditional Japanese beverages include *sake*, *choya* plum wine and Sapporo beer. If you're a novice when it comes to Japanese cuisine there are picture menus to help you; alternatively, opt for one of the set meals.

Trenta Due ⑨

Slezská 32	
✆ 2251 1720	
Ⓜ Trams 10 and 16	
Open: Mon Sat 1100–2400, Sun 1700–2400	
Reservations unnecessary	
No credit cards accepted	
International	

€€

You'll find this cosy cellar restaurant at the end of a courtyard. Popular with Czech diners (especially at lunchtimes), the menu can be divided roughly into Italian risotto and pasta dishes and Mexican specialities: tacos, enchiladas, *fajitas*, spicy salmon and shellfish. The salmon tends to be over-soused but the chilli con carne is

commendably hot and spicy. Attentive, friendly staff.

Zur Kanne ⑩

Anglická 23	
✆ 2251 4570	
Ⓜ Trams 6 and 11	
Open: daily 1100–2300	
Reservations recommended	
💳 💳	
Czech	

€€

A cut above the usual pub restaurant, Zur Kanne has a warm, cosy ambience, well-spaced-out tables and animal skins on the wall. The food is plain, whole-some and unashamedly bohemian: smoked beef tongue with olive oil and parmesan, spicy meat goulash with dumplings or the classic roast pork with sauer-kraut. Wash your meal down with a refreshing glass of Staropramen beer.

WENCESLAS SQUARE
Bars, cafés and pubs

Astoria

Na příkopě 23

Ø None available

🄼 Metro Můstek

Open: daily 0900–0100

€

Large, glass-fronted pizzeria in Rathova Pasáž. Unexceptional, but a handy lunchtime stop if you've been shopping.

Café Boulevard 🄸

Václavské náměstí 32

Ø 2415 2304

🄼 Trams 3, 9, 14 and 24

Open: Mon–Fri 1000–2400, Sat–Sun 0800–2400

€

French-style café with a huge glass-covered terrace, cane chairs, plant décor and an outlook on to Wenceslas Square. Specialities include pancakes (savoury and sweet).

Café de Colombia 🄳

Na příkopě 8

Ø None available

🄼 Metro Můstek

Open: daily 0800–2200

€

The appetising menu includes sweet and savoury pancakes, waffles, apple strudels, croissants, sandwiches and toasts.

Castello 🄸

Václavské náměstí 20

Ø 2422 8388

🄼 Metro Můstek

Open: daily 1100–2300

All credit cards accepted

€€

Pleasant cellar restaurant on Wenceslas Square serving pizzas, pastas, risotto and other Italian dishes.

Černá Růže Pasáž 🄸

Na příkopě 12

Ø None available

🄼 Metro Můstek

Open: daily 0900–2100

The 'Black Rose' passage is off one of Prague's main shopping streets. Facilities include: 1st floor – **Café Christian**; 2nd floor – **Bondi Bar**; Ground floor – garden **Kavárna** and **Café Bonjour** (breakfast menu 0800–1100); also a bakery selling cakes and pastries.

Concordia 🄸

Náměstí míru 3

Ø 2251 9849

🄼 Metro Náměstí míru

Open: Mon–Sat 1100–2330

€€

This smart Italian eatery with gilded mirrors, plants and wooden furnishings overlooks the square. The menu comprises pizzas, soups, risotto dishes and meat grills.

Hostinec U Hrocha 🄸

Slezská 26

Ø None available

🄼 Trams 10 and 16

Open: Mon–Fri 1030–2300 Sat 1100–2300, Sun 1100–2130

€

Typical Czech beer hall, dispensing Krušovice on draught. Lunchtime specialities include pork, boiled beef, Chinese and fish dishes.

Koruna Pasáž 🄸

Václavské náměstí 6

Ø 2447 4044

🄼 Metro Můstek

Open: daily 0700–0100

The 'Koruna House' was designed in 1911 by modernist architect Antonín Pfeiffer, and boasts a stunning glass roof. The renovated interior is now full of boutiques and glass-fronted eateries with tables spilling into the passage. (The echoing disco music can be intrusive). **Café Kenvelo** (first floor) offers Italian and American specialties including pizzas, pasta dishes, grills, and the 'greatest salads in Prague'. The downstairs café serves filled rolls, sandwiches and fast food. Breakfast menus are also available.

Pivnice ⑲

Budečská 40
∅ None available
🚊 Tram 11
Open: Mon–Fri 1100–2400, Sat 1600–2400, Sun 1600–2200
💰💰

Humorous pseudo-medieval wall paintings enliven this modern Czech pub, which attracts a predominantly youthful clientele. Moravian wines are served, as well as beer and pub grub.

Pizzeria Venezia ⑳

Anglická 9
∅ 2423 7461
🚊 Trams 6 and 11
Open: daily 0900–2300
💰💰

Look out for the eye-catching orange building near náměstí míru. Inside, the décor is pleasing if unassuming – plain wooden tables in a green enclosure, decorated with mock gondola mooring posts. Apart from an excellent selection of pizzas, there's lasagne, spaghetti and other pasta dishes, as well as soups, salads and *antipasti*, all reasonably priced (10 per cent discount for children at weekends). Ham and egg breakfasts are served until 1100.

Pod Smetankou ㉑

Mánesova 7
∅ 2423 0043
🚊 Tram 11
Open: Mon–Fri 1000–2400, Sat–Sun 1100–2300
💰

This Czech local offers five different beers including Gambrinus, Pilsner Urquell and Budweiser and also pork and other traditional Czech dishes. There's a billiard table too.

La Tonnelle ㉒

Anny Letenské 18
∅ 2225 3690
🚊 Tram 11
Open: Mon–Fri 1130–2400, Sat 1700–2400
💰💰

This French wine bar has enjoyed a lot of media attention of late. The décor is plain and unobtrusive, the music suitably Gallic and the vintage wines (served by the glass or bottle) super-abundant. Cheese or meat platters are on hand to stimulate the palate.

Velvet ㉓

Října 28, corner of Václavské náměstí
∅ None available
🚊 Metro Můstek
Open: daily 0900–2300
💰

'Velvet' as in Velvet Revolution – the movement which led to the demise of the Communist Party in 1989. Civic Forum, the democratic alliance headed by Václav Havel, made this building its headquarters. Now it's a cocktail bar with a glass-covered terrace overlooking Wenceslas Square.

WENCESLAS SQUARE
Shops, markets and picnic sites

Bakeries and confectioners

Cukrárna ㉔

Václavské náměstí 27

Ⓜ Metro Můstek

Open: Mon 1200–2000,
Tue–Sun 1000–2000

Small, modern pastry shop offering a choice of pancakes, cakes, pastries and ice cream cocktails.

Cukrárna Simona ㉕

Václavské náměstí 14

Ⓜ Metro Můstek

Open: Mon–Fri 0900–2000,
Sat 1000–2000, Sun 1000–1800

Small sweet shop, full to bursting with Belgian chocolates and other delicacies, including Czech liqueurs – Becherovka, Slivovice and Kokos.

Dobrá Čajovna ㉖

Václavské náměstí 14

Ⓜ Metro Můstek

Open: Mon–Sat 1000–2130,
Sun 1500–2130

Tiny tea shop in a small courtyard with cane chairs and a tea chest serving as a table. Craft shop next door.

Paris-Praha ㉗

Jindřišská 7

Ⓣ Trams 3, 9, 14 and 24

Open: daily 0900–1900

This patisserie near **Fruits de France** (*see below*) offers quality salads, roulades and cheeses, as well as doughnuts, pastries, croissants and filled rolls. There's a small café at the back.

Grocers and supermarkets

E Kliment ㉘

Václavské náměstí 39

Ⓣ Trams 3, 9, 14 and 24

Open: Mon–Fri 0800–1900

You'll find this meat delicatessen next to the Pasaž Jiřího Grossmanna. Apart from the usual line in sausages and cooked meat, there are salads, a little cheese, filled rolls, soft drinks and grilled chicken.

Fruits de France ㉙

Jindřišská 9 and
Bělehradská 94

Ⓣ Trams 3, 9, 14 and 24

Open: daily

This store specialising in French produce has become so popular that there's now a second branch. The fruit and vegetables include rarities such as passion fruits and seedless grapes while the deli counter is out of this world (French hams and cheeses, escargots, smoked duck, home-made pâtés, tapenades and canapés). There's also a fine selection of wines and oils.

Julius Meinl ㉚

28 Října 9

Ⓜ Metro Můstek

Open: Mon–Fri 0700–2000,
Sat 0700–1400

Food department on the ground floor as you go in.

Julius Meinl ㉛

Bílá Labut', Václavské
náměstí 59

Ⓜ Metro Muzeum

Open: Mon–Fri 0800–1900,
Sat 0800–1800

Supermarket on the first floor of department store.

Julius Meinl ㉜

Krone, Václavské náměstí 21

Ⓜ Metro Můstek

Open: Mon–Fri 0900–2000,
Sat 0900–1900, Sun 1000–1800

Supermarket on the ground floor of a department store. This branch has a good deli counter and a café selling soups, sandwiches and pastries. The entrance is by the metro.

▲ Delicatessen at Julius Meinl

Koloniál U Jirsů 🟢

Náměstí míru

🔘 Metro Náměstí míru

Open: Mon–Fri 0800–2100

This typical Czech corner shop sells fresh rolls, cheeses, pastries, bread and alcoholic and other drinks.

Občerstvení 🟢

Václavské náměstí

🔘 Metro Můstek or Muzeum

Open: all day and late into the evening

This is a generic name for the fast food kiosk. There are at least half a dozen on Wenceslas Square, selling hot dogs, baguettes, burgers, sandwiches, chicken pieces, corn on the cob, soft drinks and alcohol.

Pomona Market 🟢

Václavské náměstí 54, corner of Ve Smečkách

🔘 Metro Muzeum

Open: Mon–Fri 0700–2100, Sat 0900–2100, Sun 1200–2100

Supermarket-style grocery store with bakery and delicatessen counter. The stall outside sells fresh fruit.

Vinohradská Pavilon 🟢

Vinohradská 50

🔘 Tram 11

Open: Mon–Fri 0900–2100, Sun 1200–1800

This stunning neo-Renaissance market hall, made from glazed iron, was designed by Antonín Turek in around 1900. Comprehensive renovation was completed in 1995 when the Vinohradská Pavilon received the European shopping centre of the year award. You'll find a branch of Julius Meinl on the lower ground floor and the M&M café bar up the escalator on the first floor.

Zemark 🟢

Václavské náměstí 42

🔘 Metro Můstek

Open: Mon–Sat 0800–2100, Sun 1200–2100

Comprehensive delicatessen with a prime site on Wenceslas Square. Apart from meats and cheeses, there's a wonderful array of salads, an excellent choice of Moravian wines (such as Riezlink Vlašský and Rulandské Modre) and also whiskies and liqueurs.

Wines

Prodej Sudového Vína Artur 🟢

Anglická 17

🔘 Metro Náměstí míru

Open: Mon–Sat 1100–1900

Wine shop with a small selection of Moravian, Frankovka, Riezlink and Müller-Thurgau wines, among others. Tastings are by the glass.

Picnic sites

Náměstí míru 🟢

🔘 Metro Náměstí míru

A small square in front of St Ludmilla's Church. Not much incentive to linger here, more a place to rest your legs.

Riegrovy sady 🟢

Polská

🔘 Tram 11

This modest local park overlooks the city from Vinohrady (Vineyard Hills).

Obecní Dům

The monument to art nouveau

One of Europe's finest art-nouveau monuments, Prague's Municipal House or 'People's House' was completed in 1911, eight years after Antonín Balšánek and Osvald Polívka won an open competition for the design. The building occupies the site of the King's Court, a royal palace close to the fortified walls of the Old Town built in the 14th century by Wenceslas IV. Obecní Dům represents a flowering of the Czech national revival, cultural as well as architectural. It was from here that President Tomáš Masaryk announced the founding of the Independent State of Czechoslovakia in October 1918.

The Municipal House was a model civic centre, containing offices, concert halls and assembly rooms, as well as cafés, bars and restaurants. The cream of Prague's artistic community, including such eminent talents as Alfons Mucha, Karel Špillar and Ladislav Šaloun were recruited to assist with the project and all of them have left their mark on the stunning building – Špillar, for example, was responsible for the eye-catching mosaic on the façade, entitled *The Apotheosis of Prague*. In 1997 Obecní Dům reopened after a thorough renovation. While there is an overall unity of design and purpose, each room is conceived as a self-contained work of art. Now visitors can once again appreciate every detail of this dazzling achievement, an eclectic composite of sculptures, paintings, stained glass, wrought-iron work, mosaics, tiling, wood carving and stucco. Highlights include the Mayor's Room, with paintings by Alfons Mucha.

Classical concerts are held in the Smetana Hall, home of the Prague Symphony Orchestra. Sculptures by Šaloun, frescos of the Muses by Špillar, portraits of the composers by Kalvoda and wood carvings by Navrátil decorate the sumptuous interior.

For orientation purposes, it's best to start with the cultural and information centre on the upper ground floor which organises guided tours of the building, ticket sales for concerts, exhibitions and social events and the sale of postcards, CDs, catalogues, books about Prague, souvenirs and original art works (open: 1000–1800).

▲ Painting in French restaurant

Places to eat in Obecní Dům (⊙ *metro Náměstí Republiky*):

- **American bar** *Basement (opposite the Pilsen restaurant).* The central light fitting in painted glass is by Křižík. Also note the drawings on eating and drinking themes.
- **Café** *Ground floor; open: daily 1000–2200;* ❶–❶❷. The décor includes mahogany partitions and tables with leather-covered benches. Note the Nymph Fountain with marble relief by Josef Pekárek. Waiters dressed in pale green and black waistcoats serve light refreshments.
- **French restaurant** *Ground floor, ✆ 2200 2777; open: daily 1200–1500, 1800–2300 (Sat until 2400); reservations essential; all credit cards accepted; International;* ❷❷–❷❷❸. The interior decoration comprises

▲ Waiter at Obecní Dům

> An eclectic composite of sculptures, paintings, stained glass, wrought-iron work, mosaics, tiling, wood carving and stucco.

sumptuous allegorical paintings, art-nouveau murals, gilded chandeliers, wooden wainscoting, and a lustrous clock suspended in an ethereal frame. Note the allegorical wall painting 'Prague welcoming its visitors' by Josef Wenig on the side wall. During the renovation the original wallpaper was discovered and has also been restored.

There are several menus: á la carte, gourmet (menu *dégustation*) and 'surprise' (seven courses selected by the chef). Recommended first courses are salmon mousse with marinated courgettes, breast of chicken in maple syrup, chicken liver noodles and cream of asparagus, lobster or cold strawberry soups. Follow this either with a fish course or with a meat main meal such as fresh quail served Swiss-style with ratatouille, potato *gnocchi* and basil sauce, half duck with red cabbage, dumplings and almond stuffing, veal schnitzel with asparagus tips, beef stroganoff, or grilled Australian lamb fillets in a rose hip and port sauce.

- **Plzenska restaurant** *In the basement; ✆ 2200 2780; open: daily 1100–2330; reservations unnecessary; all credit cards accepted; Czech;* ❶❷. Restored from original plans and drawings, the Pilsen restaurant is a cavernous dining room in the style of a beer keller. The theme is the fruits of the harvest and features a vivid ceramic mosaic by Jakub Obrovský, *Harvest in Bohemia*, flanked by coloured tiles and stained glass, decorated with fruit and corn motifs.

Nerudova of the Lesser Town

It's a steep climb to the top of Nerudova, as tourists heading for Prague Castle soon discover. Almost every other building is a café or restaurant, each with its own eye-catching house sign. The lunch menus are good value here, but the afternoon teas and ice creams are a little pricey.

STRAHOVSKÝ KLÁŠTER PICTUR GALLERY

NERUDOVA OF THE LESSER TOWN
Restaurants

Ada ❶

Hotel Hoffmeister, Pod Bruskou 7

☎ 5101 7133

🚇 Metro Malostranská; trams 18 and 22

Open: daily 1100–1500, 1830–2330

Reservations recommended

All credit cards accepted

Czech-French

❶❶❶

This is a restaurant that sets out to impress. Everything is just-so: immaculate place settings, flowers on the table, waiters formally attired in dinner jackets and black ties and views across the hillside gardens of the Lesser Town. The food is nouvelle cuisine at its best – baked pigeon in wild sauce with roasted veal sweetbread; Zander 'bonne femme' with baby carrots; pancakes and cinnamon ice cream. Czech beers are available on draught, as well as a selection of French and Moravian wines.

Bazaar Mediterranée ❷

Nerudova 40

☎ 9005 4510

🚇 Metro Malostranská

Open: daily 1100–2400

Reservations essential

All credit cards accepted

Mediterranean

❶❶❶

Hip eatery with shades of the kasbah in a

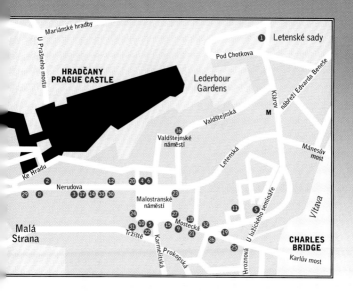

menu which features couscous and Moroccan stews, alongside oysters and coq au vin. The dimly lit dining area suggests intimacy and romance but, when the garden opens in the summer and the music bar gets into its stride, forget it.

U Bonaparta ❸

Nerudova 29

☎ 5753 1225

Ⓜ Metro Malostranská

Open: daily 1100–2400

Reservations recommended

All credit cards accepted

International

❻❻

Of the dozens of restaurants on Nerudova,

Bonaparte's has always been one of the most popular. Warm and welcoming, it offers a choice of seven set menus, including Japanese fare, so there really is something for everyone – try fried crab claws with spicy sauce and entrecôte with fried egg and ham.

Černý orel ❹

Malostranské náměstí 14 (entrance on Zámecká)

☎ 536 373

Ⓜ Trams 12 and 22

Open: daily 1100–2300

Reservations recommended

All credit cards accepted

Czech-International

❻❻

The 'Black Eagle' has an interesting history. Mozart stayed here in the 18th century during one of his barnstorming visits to Prague. The house then became a pharmacy and was later the haunt of Prague artists, one of whom, Mikuláš Aleš, supplied the sgraffito decoration. The menu includes snails in Burgundy and shark steak, as well as the usual range of meat dishes.

Čertovka ❺

U lužického semináře 24

☎ 538 853

Ⓜ Metro Malostranská

Open: daily 1130–2330

Reservations recommended

Restaurant - Club Černý orel

All credit cards accepted

Czech

ⓒⓒⓒ

The restaurant takes its name from the Čertovka (Devil's Stream) which separates Kampa Island from the Lesser Town. According to legend, the devil in question was a bad-tempered woman who lived nearby. With water mills, swans, riverside gardens and views of the Charles Bridge it's a picturesque, near idyllic, corner of Prague. Understandably, the terrace attracts huge numbers of visitors during the summer – booking isn't allowed so it's a case of first come, first served.

Circle Line ⑥

Malostranské náměstí 12

✆ 5753 0021–3

🚋 Trams 12 and 22

Open: Mon–Fri 1200–2300,
Sat 1100–2300

French-Continental

ⓒⓒ–ⓒⓒⓒ

This gourmet brasserie (from the same stable as **V Zátíší** – *see page 21*) caters primarily, though not exclusively, to fish lovers. The ambience is refined, the food, out of this world. To start, try the oysters or the yellow-fin tuna carpaccio, with maybe the salmon in marinade to follow. The two set brunch menus, served from 1200 to 1800 Monday to Friday and from 1200 Saturday and Sunday, are excellent value.

U Císařů ⑦

Loretánská 175/5

✆ 2051 2079

🚋 Tram 22

Open: daily 1100–2400;
wine cellar until 0100

Reservations recommended

All credit cards accepted

Czech

ⓒⓒ

Candlelit tables, oil paintings and high-backed chairs set the scene in this elegant restaurant and *vinárna* on the crown of Castle Hill. Culinary treats include rabbit, sautéed in white wine with cream, ginger and mushrooms. The *vinárna* is downstairs in the cellar.

Dům U Červeného Lva ⑧

Nerudova 41

✆ 5753 3832–3

🚇 Metro Malostranská

Open: daily 0700–2300

Reservations recommended

All credit cards accepted

Czech

ⓒⓒ

'The House at the Red Lion' – note the sculpted emblem above the entrance – dates from the 15th century and was once the home of Prague's most celebrated painter of altar-pieces, Peter Brandl. The rambling interior (surprisingly light and airy) is full of period charm, from the gothic cellar to the Renaissance ceiling complete with painted roof beams. There are two set lunch menus, while the à la carte menu is strong on game and river fish.

Makarská ⑨

Malostranské náměstí 2
✆ 5753 0259
ⓣ Trams 12 and 22
Open: daily 1200–2400
Reservations recommended
All credit cards accepted
Czech
❶❶

Small, candlelit restaurant with a handsome wood panelled interior complete with stained-glass windows. The Czech dishes include standards such as cabbage soup with mushrooms, Bohemian carp with anchovies and boar steak on juniper berries with cranberry sauce – all very appetising. The piano bar opens at 1930.

U Mecenáše ⑩

Malostranské náměstí 10
✆ 5753 1631
ⓣ Trams 12 and 22
Open: daily 1200–2330
Reservations recommended
All credit cards accepted
Czech
❶❶❶

'The House of the Golden Lion', its original 15th-century façade still intact, enjoys a prime location on Lesser Town Square. The interior décor – stained-glass windows, dark wood panelling and brocades – is a little on the gloomy side but you can eat well here, whether you opt for the meat or fish courses. The chef's special expertise is flambée.

U Patrona ⑪

Dražického náměstí 4
✆ 531 512
ⓜ Metro Malostranská
Open: Mon–Sat 1800–2300
Reservations essential
All credit cards accepted
Czech-International
❶❶❶

Located in a charming square just off the Charles Bridge, this diminutive restaurant was at the cutting edge of the Prague culinary revolution which began after 1989. The service is as impeccable as the cooking. The menu ranges widely, from spinach and tomato soup, or homemade ravioli with shrimp and peppercorn sauce, to grilled scallops, or John Dory with leeks and courgettes.

U Tří Housliček ⑫

Nerudova 12
✆ 535 011
ⓜ Metro Malostranská
Open: daily 1130–2400

▲ U Tří Housliček

Reservations recommended

All credit cards accepted

Czech

❸ ❸

The original owner of the house was Bartolomeus Spranger, a leading court painter at the end of the 16th century. In 1681 a violinmaker by the name of Linhart Brater opened a workshop which soon acquired the name 'At the Three Fiddles'. Popular with tourists, the restaurant has a welcoming, if slightly formal, ambience suggested by the classical music playing in the background. The culinary strengths are the game dishes – venison, red deer and boar are all available, with fish on offer if you're averse to meat. The set menus are good value and include at least one vegetarian dish.

U Zlaté Hrušky ⑬

Nový Svět 3

∅ 2051 4778

🚋 Tram 22

Open: daily 1130–1500, 1800–2400

Reservations essential

▮▮▮ ●● American Express

International

❸ ❸ ❸

'At the Golden Pear' enjoys a romantic setting on a lane called 'New World' and is one of a line of 17th-century cottages. The astronomer Tycho Brahe lived at number one. Long a favourite with the Czech president, the international menu leans towards game dishes – the venison is especially recommended.

NERUDOVA OF THE LESSER TOWN

Bars, cafés and pubs

Arcimboldo/Rudolf II

Nerudova 13

✆ 5753 2558

Ⓜ Metro Malostranská

Open: daily 1100–2300

€€

A good lunch stop if you can find a table. The restaurant specialises in game dishes such as rabbit and bacon stew, deer steak on grapes and wild boar in rose hip sauce – the tourist menu includes chicken and chips. Other plusses are the garden terrace and the traditional Czech pub downstairs.

Bílý Orel

Malostranské náměstí 4

Ⓝ None available

Ⓣ Trams 12 and 22

Open: daily 0800–2300

€€

Also known as 'Zum Weissen Adler', 'At the White Eagle' was once a pharmacy. Today it's a pleasant, if small, café-bar offering hearty Czech fare along the lines of grilled knuckle of pig and the ubiquitous roast pork with cabbage and dumplings. Sandwiches and salads are on standby for the faint-hearted.

Café Ledebour

Valdštejnské náměstí 3

✆ 5701 0412

Ⓜ Metro Malostranská

Open: daily 1100–2200

€€

The coaching house of the old Ledebour Palace is now an attractive café with a painted baroque ceiling. The pavilion in the neighbouring terraced garden was designed in the early 18th century by the distinguished Italian architect, Giovanni Battista Alliprandi.

Caffè-Ristorante Italia

Nerudova 17

✆ 530 386

Ⓜ Metro Malostranská

Open: daily 0900–2300

€€

Italian eatery with a prime location on the charming street leading to Prague Castle. Each of the small rooms has its own domestic feel. Service is courteous and attentive, though the food is nothing to write home about. The best value is the two-course tourist menu.

Canzone

Josefska 2

✆ 5731 9894

Ⓣ Trams 12 and 22

Open: daily 1100–2300

€€

▲ Bílý Orel

Inviting pizzeria close to the Charles Bridge. A predictable range of pizza toppings and pasta dishes can all be washed down by Krušovice beer.

U Černého Beránka  ⑲

Mostecká 8

∅ None available

🚃 Trams 12 and 22

Open: daily 0800–2100

Ⓒ

The snack bar 'At the Black Lamb' serves a tasty selection of pancakes, toasted sandwiches and omelettes.

U Čerta ⑳

Nerudova 4

∅ 5753 1526

Ⓜ Metro Malostranská

Open: daily 1100–2300

ⒸⒸ

'At the Devil's' greets its customers with a giant effigy of suitably menacing appearance. The menu features game specialities such as

▲ Malostranská Kavárna

venison, boar and rabbit.

Chiméra ㉑

Lázeňská 6

∅ None available

🚃 Trams 12 and 22

Open: daily 1200–2300

Ⓒ

Picturesquely situated near the Maltese Church, this café has its own loyal clientele, but welcomes newcomers. Settle back into one of the armchairs with a coffee or a glass of Jack Daniels and put the sightseeing schedule on hold for a while.

J J Murphys & Co ㉒

Tržiště 4

∅ 5753 0018

🚃 Trams 12 and 22

Open: daily 1000–2400

Ⓒ–ⒸⒸ

Irish pub doling out cocktails and single malts as well as the flagship Murphys stout. Live music on Fridays and brunch served on Saturday and Sunday.

Malostranská Beseda ㉓

Malostranské náměstí 21

∅ 535 528

🚃 Trams 12 and 22

Open: daily 1000–2400

ⒸⒸ

The word *beseda* implies friendly conversation and this modern café, overlooking Lesser Town Square, has all the right vibes, especially if you

can get a table in the arcade overlooking St Nicholas' Church.

Malostranská Kavárna ㉔

Malostranské náměstí 5

∅ 533 092

🚃 Trams 12 and 22

Open: daily 0900–1100

Ⓒ

This café with a soothing, restful ambience was the haunt in times gone by of Austrian army officers.

U Mostecké Věže ㉕

Mostecká 3

∅ 536 635

🚃 Trams 12 and 22

Open: daily 1000–2200

Ⓒ

Café near the Charles Bridge with small garden terrace and appetising menu – everything from chicken fondue to ham platters and chicken salads.

U Snědeného Krámu ㉖

Mostecká 5/Lázeňská 19

∅ 531 795

🚃 Trams 12 and 22

Open: daily 1200–2300

ⒸⒸ

This atmospheric pub near the Charles Bridge dates from the turn of the last century and dishes up Bohemian kitchen fare. There are four beers to choose from: Pilsner Urquell, Budweiser-Budvar, Gambrinus and the dark Purkmistr.

NERUDOVA OF THE LESSER TOWN
Shops, markets and picnic sites

Bakeries and confectioners

Cukrárna U Sv. Mikuláše ㉗

Malostranské náměstí 9

Ⓣ Trams 12 and 22

Open: Sun–Thu 1000–1830, Fri–Sat 1000–2000

Confectioners near St Nicholas' Church also dispensing freshly squeezed fruit juices.

Mikulaše ㉗

Malostranské náměstí 9

Ⓣ Trams 12 and 22

Open: Mon–Thu 1000–1800, Fri–Sun 1000–1900

Sweet shop and patisserie selling filled rolls and salads, as well as the usual cakes and pastries. There's a small seating area if you want to eat in.

U Tří Kupeství Sekyrek ㉘

Úvoz 6

Ⓣ Tram 22

Open: Mon–Fri 0730–2000, Sat–Sun 1000–1800

Enticing patisserie with a sideline in bread rolls and Czech wines. Small deli counter.

Grocers

Asena ㉙

Úvoz 1, also at Pod Krejcárkem 975, Prague 3

Ⓣ Tram 22

Open: daily 0800–2000

A Turkish emporium is the last thing you'd expect to find in the vicinity of Prague Castle, nevertheless, here it is. You can stop here for a glass of Turkish tea while feasting your eyes on the enticing displays of *lokum* (Turkish delight), sweetmeats and preserves.

Malostranská Samoobsluha ㉚

Nerudova 9

Ⓜ Metro Malostranská

Open: Mon–Fri, 0700–2000, Sat 1000–2000, Sun 1100–2000

'Malostrana Supermarket' is a useful shop with an excellent location on the road leading to Prague Castle. Apart from an extensive range of groceries, there's a delicatessen and a fast food service delivering grilled chicken, hot dogs, potatoes, salads and baguettes.

Ovoce a Zelenina ㉛

Tržiště 10

Ⓣ Trams 12 and 22

Open: Mon–Fri 0730–2000, Sat 1000–1800, Sun 1100–1400

The name says it all – fruit and vegetables in large quantities. You will also find soft and alcoholic beverages.

Potraviny A Lahůdky ㉜

Mostecká 28

Ⓣ Trams 12 and 22

Open: Mon–Fri 0700–2200, Sat 0800–2200, Sun 0900–2200

Just beyond the Charles Bridge, 'Groceries and Dairy Produce' delivers more than it promises: scrumptious filled rolls and salads, gift-wrapped sweets and chocolates, biscuits, nuts, Czech liqueurs and wines.

U Zeleného Čaje ㉝

Nerudova 19

Ⓜ Metro Malostranská

Open: daily 1100–2200

'At the Green Tea' carries the pervasive scent of Darjeeling and other exotic destinations. The café next door sells fruit and aromatic varieties, as well as sandwiches and Moravian wines.

Italian restaurants

A slice of Italia

From the sophisticated *ristorante* to the humble pizzeria, Prague has something to offer every devotee of Italian cooking.

• **Don Giovanni** *Karolíny Světlé 34, Karlova; ∅ 2222 2062;* ⓜ *metro Staroměstská; open: daily 1200–2400; reservations essential; all credit cards accepted;* ❶❷❸. One of the finest Italian restaurants in town, Don Giovanni prides itself on using only authentic, home-grown ingredients. It's in a prime location, with views towards the Charles Bridge and the Lesser Town. The cooking too is *sans pareil.* Try the *bruschetta* with olive oil and tomatoes as a starter (scrumptious) or the spinach pancake au gratin. The *pappardelle,* served *al dente* with shrimps, tomato, bacon and rucola salad is outstanding among the pasta dishes.

• **Kmotra** *V Jirchářích 12, Národní Třída; ∅ 2491 5809;* ⓜ *metro Národní Třída; open: daily 1100–0100; reservations not allowed; no credit cards accepted;* ❶❷. Where 'Godmother' gets its name from is anyone's guess.

What is certain is that its reputation for dreamy pizza toppings is well deserved. Sadly this means queues out into the street during summer – if it's any consolation, there's a fast customer turnover. Expect to share tables.

• **Modrá zahrada** *Pařížská 14, Celetná; ∅ 232 7171;* ⓜ *metro Staroměstská; open: daily 1100–2400; reservations recommended; no credit cards accepted;* ❶❷. Located on one of Prague's most fashionable (and imposing) streets, the 'Blue Garden' is a reliable, very busy pizzeria with a menu as long as your arm. The salads, too, are fresh and excellent value. A takeaway service is available.

• **Pasta Fresca** *Celetná 11/ Mánesova 59, Wenceslas Square; ∅ 2423 0244/627 5913;* ⓜ *metro Náměstí Republiky/tram 11; open: daily 1100–2400; reservations unnecessary; all credit cards accepted;* ❶❷. Informality is the trade mark of the Ambiente chain, and judging by the popularity of their restaurants, they've got it off to a fine art (tables are at a premium at peak times). The Celetná branch is handy for visiting Obecní Dům and other Old Town sights, and boasts a pancake bar, open from 0900. Apart from crêpes and pasta dishes, the specialities include barbecued ribs and steaks.

• **Al Pavone** *Moskevská 56, Národní Třída; ☎ 7172 0019;* Ⓜ *metro Národní Třída; open: daily 1100–2300; reservations recommended; all credit cards accepted;* ⓞⓞ. Warm and inviting in the evenings when the bright décor is softened by candlelight, the kitchen here uses only authentic ingredients, imported directly from Italy. That said, the pizzas, though cooked the traditional way in a wood-fired oven, are nothing to write home about. Better to opt for the cannelloni or another of the pasta dishes as a main course, and start either with the soup (cream of broccoli with salmon) or the *calamari fritti* (fried squid).

• **Pizzeria Azzurra** *Dlouhá 35, Celetná; ☎ 2481 5613;* Ⓜ *metro Náměstí Republiky; open: daily 1100–2300; reservations recommended; no credit cards accepted;* ⓞⓞ. Regular pizzeria, tempting customers off the street with heavenly aromas and an excellent choice of toppings. Other dishes include lasagne, spaghetti, risotto, chicken, omelettes and fresh salads.

• **Pizzeria Rugantino** *Dusní 4; ☎ 231 8172;* Ⓜ *metro Staroměstská; open: Mon–Sat 1100–2300, Sun 1800– 2300; reservations recommended; all credit cards accepted;* ⓞⓞ. With fifty genuine Neapolitan pizza choices at the last time of asking, you could spend all day here studying the menu – they gain full marks for including more than a dozen vegetarian toppings. If you're not in the mood for a

▲ Tuna and swordfish carpaccio

pizza, don't despair, the pasta dishes and whopping salads are just as tempting.

• **San Pietro 1** (and San Pietro III); *Benediktská 16/Dlouhá 8, Celetná; ☎ 2482 6365/231 0018;* Ⓜ *metro Náměstí Republiky; open: daily 1100–2300; reservations recommended; all credit cards accepted;* ⓞⓞ. Pizza chain run by locals Petr and Zdena Mikulka. The cheery décor features plants, tasteful prints and brightly painted walls. You'll find a large choice of pizzas and friendly, welcoming staff. (*See also page 63.*)

• **Tosca** *Hradčanské náměstí 5, Nerudova; ☎ 1051 6020;* Ⓜ *metro Malostranská; open: wine cellar daily 1200–1500, 1800–0100; restaurant daily 1000–2200; reservations recommended; all credit cards accepted;* ⓞⓞ. The baroque Tuscany Palace takes its name from the Duke of Tuscany who acquired it in 1718 – you can see his sculptured coat of arms above the twin-columned portals. It's one of the loveliest buildings in Hradčany and a great location for a restaurant, best appreciated if you can grab a table under the arcade or in the garden (*open: Apr–Oct*).

> **The pappardelle, served al dente with shrimps, tomato, bacon and rucola salad, is outstanding.**

Holešovice

Perfect for picnics, this area north of the River Vltava includes the Letná Gardens and Stromovka, a park that was once a royal hunting ground. Tourists visiting the National Gallery of Modern Art will notice how cafés, bars and pizzerias are mushrooming on Dukelských hrdinů.

HOLEŠOVICE
Restaurants

Aqua ❶

U Plovárny

✆ 5731 2578

🚊 Tram 12

Open: 1730–0100; kitchen 1800–2315

Reservations essential

All credit cards accepted

International

❷❷–❷❷❷

This recently converted, elegant, neo-classical building was built as a spa and baths in the 1890s; the location is a lovely riverside one, opposite the Hotel Intercontinental. The restaurant specialises in grills and seafood, with a buffet on Thursdays from 1900 and barbecues on the terrace in the summer.

Café Dante ❷

Dukelských hrdinů 16

✆ 870 193

🚊 Trams 5, 12 and 17

Open: Mon–Fri 0800–2200, Sat–Sun 1100–2200

Reservations unnecessary

No credit cards accepted

Italian-Czech

❷❷

An attractive Italian eatery occupying a prime site on the main shopping street of Holešovice. Pizzas, calzone, risotto and pasta dishes are complemented with an appetising salad buffet. Most of the starters (such as chicken cocktail with mushrooms) and some main courses have a Czech orientation, presumably to suit the middle-aged clientele.

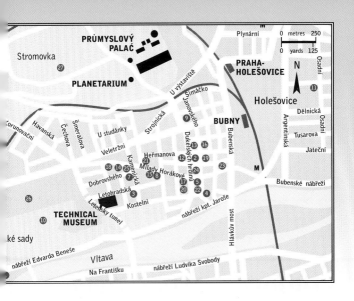

▲ Salmon and John Dory

▲ Hanavský Pavilon

Capri ❸

Kamenická 23

✆ 3337 9306

🚊 Trams 1, 8, 25 and 26

Open: daily 1030–2400

Reservations unnecessary

No credit cards accepted

Italian

💰💰

A pleasant neighbourhood restaurant with a good line in pizzas (twenty toppings to choose from), pastas, steaks and chicken dishes such as *pollo alla cacciatora*.

La Crêperie ❹

Janovského 4

✆ 878 040

🚊 Trams 5, 12 and 17

Open: Mon–Sat 1200–2300

Reservations recommended

All credit cards accepted

French

💰💰

Swish French pancake house with a cosy atmosphere, not far from the Veletržní Palác (National Gallery of Modern Art). There's a mouth-watering choice of fillings.

Domažlická Jizba ❺

Strossmayerovo náměstí 2

✆ 879 083

🚊 Metro Vltavská; trams 1, 5, 8, 12, 17, 25 and 26

Open: daily 1130–0030

Reservations unnecessary

💳 💰

Czech

💰

Not far from Holešovice station and St Antonín's Church – a local landmark – this neighbourhood diner serves a range of typical bohemian dishes, including grilled meats and freshwater fish. Krušovice lager is available on draught.

Hanavský Pavilon

Letenské sady 173	
✆ 325 792	
🚊 Tram 12	
Open: daily 1130–2400	
Reservations recommended	
All credit cards accepted	
Czech	
🅒🅒🅒	

The pavilion in Letná Park is a cast-iron neo-baroque folly, created for the Jubilee Exhibition of 1891. Snacks, soft drinks and Krušovice beer are served on the terrace and more formal meals inside. Enjoy fabulous views of the castle and the Lesser Town.

Hostinec Na Staré Kovárně V Bráníku ➐

Kamenická 17	
✆ 3337 7126	
🚊 Trams 1, 8, 25 and 26	
Open: Mon–Sat 1100–0100, Sun 1130–2330	
Reservations recommended	
No credit cards accepted	
Czech-International	
🅒🅒	

Slightly off the beaten track, this quirky, faintly amusing pub-restaurant is remarkable for its off-beat décor. Note the motor bike hanging from the ceiling and the discarded coins glued to the floor. The dishes (grilled meats, fish

fillets, chilli con carne and so on) are named after celebrities past and present but are otherwise unremarkable. More to most people's liking is the availability of Radegast beer on draught.

Hotel Belvedere ➑

Milady Horákové 17	
✆ 2010 611	
🚊 Trams 1, 8, 25 and 26	
Open: daily 1100–2400	
Reservations unnecessary	
All credit cards accepted	
Czech-Italian	
🅒🅒	

A convenient lunch stop if you've been visiting the National Gallery of Modern Art, the Technical Museum or the Exhibition Ground. Both the restaurant and grill section have recently been refurbished, so don't be put off by the down-at-heel exterior. The menu divides fairly evenly into Italian and Czech dishes. Of the latter, the fried carp from Třeboň can be recommended – they've been farming carp in the ponds of this southern Bohemian town since the 15th century.

Leonardo ➒

Dukelských hrdinů 42	
✆ 801 279	
🚊 Trams 5, 12 and 17	
Open: daily 1200–2400	
Reservations unnecessary	
Czech-Italian	
🅒🅒	

Modern, nicely turned-out restaurant on a busy shopping street. There's a daily tourist menu if you don't want to eat à la carte. The Czech dishes include Prague ham, roast beef, trout cooked in beer, smoked eel and the house speciality, 'Chicken Leonardo' (served with mushrooms, leeks and gin!). Budweiser-Budvar is available on draught.

Letenský Zámeček (Ullmann/Belcredi) ➓

Lentenské sady 341	
✆ 371 206	
🚊 Tram 12	
Open: daily 1130–2300	
Reservations unnecessary	
All credit cards accepted	
Czech-International	
🅒🅒	

Known variously as Restaurant Ullmann, or even Belcredi, the proper name, meaning 'Letná Chateau', is both accurate and apt. The handsome neo-Renaissance building dates from the 19th century and has a wonderful location on the upper slopes of a wooded park, with fabulous views across the city (the main reason for dining here). The food is acceptable, sometimes good. Typical main courses include wild rice risotto with seafood, or fillet of beef with dumplings or turkey breast. You could start with caviar or crab salad and round off your meal with a strudel or cheesecake. If you're a beer lover you'll enjoy the draught Velkrpovice (Kozel) lager.

Mecca ⑪

U Průhonu 3
☏ 8387 0522
Ⓜ Metro Vltavská
Open: daily 1100–0200
Reservations recommended
All credit cards accepted
International

ⓒⓒ

A newcomer to the culinary scene, Mecca is a trendy, slightly pretentious eatery catering to a motley clientele. The food more than passes muster and prices are reasonable.

Pasquale ⑫

Sochora 35
☏ 2057 0356
Ⓣ Trams 1, 8, 25 and 26
Open: Mon–Fri 1100–2300
Reservations unnecessary
All credit cards accepted
Italian

ⓒⓒ

Pasquale is an engaging modern trattoria which offers the usual range of Italian dishes. Starters include squid or salmon pâté, main courses, chicken in marsala sauce, beefsteak and grilled trout. The choice also includes pasta dishes and salads.

Pizzeria Flamengo ⑬

Dukelských hrdinů 20
☏ 6671 1345
Ⓣ Trams 5, 12 and 17
Open: daily 1000–2300
Reservations unnecessary
No credit cards accepted
Italian

ⓒ

Typical pizza joint with green, wooden shutters, brick counter and wood-fired oven. Pasta and salad dishes are also available.

U Počtú ⑭

Milady Horákové 47
☏ 370 085
Ⓣ Trams 1, 8, 25 and 26
Open: Mon–Fri 1100–2400, Sat–Sun 1700–2400
Reservations recommended
All credit cards accepted
Czech

ⓒⓒ

This small, attractively old-fashioned restaurant (just two rooms) proves handy for the National Gallery of Modern Art and the Technical Museum. The waiting staff are friendly and approachable and the food, comprising traditional Bohemian dishes, is surprisingly good considering the price. It can be a little noisy. The garlic soup and chicken livers cooked in wine come highly recommended.

Rhapsody ⑨

Dukelských hrdinů 46
☏ 806 768
Ⓣ Trams 5, 12 and 17
Open: Mon–Sat 1830–0200
Reservations recommended
All credit cards accepted
International

ⓒⓒⓒ

This classy restaurant and piano bar would deserve a mention in any food guide. The cooking has a French bent – Cancale oysters, *escargots* de Bourgogne, *foie gras* and onion soup, to mention only the starters. The main courses are equally distinguished: *filet d'agneau façon de berger, magret de canard* or, more unusually, *suprême de volaille Antillaise* (West Indian chicken curry). A perfect spot for a romantic dinner.

HOLEŠOVICE
Bars, cafés and pubs

Beer Bar ⓯

Milady Horákové 17

∅ None available

🚋 Trams 1, 8, 25 and 26

Open: daily 1100–2300

€

Opposite the Hotel Belvedere, this agreeable bar is popular with locals – not surprisingly with Pilsner Urquell available on draught.

Corso ⑨

Dukelských hrdinů 48

∅ 806 541

🚋 Trams 5, 12 and 17

Open: daily 0700–2300

All credit cards accepted

€€

On the main shopping street of Holešovice, this café-bar offers hot meals, including grilled carp and steaks (beef, salmon and tuna), and also vegetarian dishes, pancakes and strudels.

O'Brien's ⓰

Janovského 36

∅ 6671 2655

🚋 Trams 5, 12 and 17

Open: daily 1300–0100

€

Irish pub patronised mainly by Czechs and serving up the cheapest Guinness in town. Have a go on the pool table.

Orient Express Grill Bar ⓱

Milady Horákové 5

∅ 375 743

🚋 Trams 1, 8, 25 and 26

Open: daily 0800–2200

€

This fast food outlet comprises a café-bar area and takeaway counter. It serves chicken and cheese-burgers, hot dogs, hamburgers, chips and draught beer.

San Pietro II ⓲

Milady Horákové 63

∅ 3338 0259

🚋 Trams 1, 8, 25 and 26

Open: daily 1100–2300

€€

One of a chain of cafés owned by Zdena and Petr Mikulka, dishing up a large choice of pizzas, pastas and grills.

U Sv. Antonička ⓳

Sochora 12

∅ None available

🚋 Trams 1, 8, 25 and 26

Open: Mon–Fri 0900–2300, Sat–Sun 1030–2100

€

Near St Anthony's Church, hence the name. Hot dishes are served all day, consisting of snacks and plain honest fare (mainly meat and potatoes). Gambrinus beer on draught.

Uč Noské Pečivo ⓴

Dukelských hrdinů 25a

∅ None available

🚋 Trams 5, 12 and 17

Open: Mon–Fri 0800–1730

€

Prefabricated stand with a few outside tables next to the bakers at number 25, selling hot snacks, cakes and bread.

U Velblouda ㉑

Haškova 3

∅ None available

🚋 Trams 1, 8, 25 and 26

Open: daily 0800–2000

€

Small *vinárna* with takeaway service: mainly burgers, salads and Czech standards.

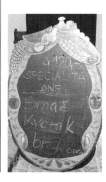

HOLEŠOVICE

Bakeries

Michelské Pekárne 20

Dukelských hrdinů 25
🚊 Trams 5, 12 and 17
Open: Mon–Fri 0700–1730,
Sun 1500–1800

An appetising bakery selling a range of Czech breads and pastries – for example *bábovka mramorova* (marble cake) and *bábovka makova* (poppy seed cake); also doughnuts, croissants, hot pasties and sausage rolls.

Confectioners

Cukrárna 22

Dukelských hrdinů 6
🚊 Trams 5, 12 and 17
Open: Mon–Fri 0800–1800,
Sat 0830–1230

Confectioners with a good range of chocolates, including Belgian pralines and the Austrian delicacy, Mozart Kugerln. You'll also find some interesting liqueurs – Bohemian pear, for example, as well as Becherovka.

Darkova-Sluzhba-Cukrovinky 23

Antonínská 7

🚇 Metro Vltavská
Open: Mon–Fri 0900–1800,
Sat 1000–1430, Sun 1230–1530

This handy sweet shop, just a few steps away from the metro station and tram stops, specialises in gift-wrapped chocolates, liqueurs and Czech sparkling wine (Bohemia Sekt).

Grocers

La Festa 13

Dukelských hrdinů 18
🚊 Trams 5, 12 and 17
Open: Mon–Fri 0700–1800,
Sat 0800–1300, Sun 0900–1300

A large general store with fresh fruit and vegetables, drinks and lots more.

Lahůdky 2

Dukelských hrdinů 14
🚊 Trams 5, 12 and 17
Open: Mon–Fri 0700–1800,
Sat 0730–1130

Dairy and delicatessen where you'll also find fresh bread and croissants.

Napoje 24

Sochora 15
🚊 Trams 1, 8, 25 and 26
Open: Mon–Fri 0900–2000,
Sat 1400–2000, Sun 1600–2000

Alcoholic beverages and soft drinks (including milk) as well as pre-wrapped sandwiches are all on offer.

Ovoce a Zelenina 17

Milady Horákové 5
🚊 Trams 1, 8, 25 and 26
Open: Mon–Fri 0800–1800,
Sat 0800–1200

Among the fruit and vegetable displays you'll come across miniature bottles of Bohemia Sekt (sparkling wine).

Ryby drůbež 25

Milady Horákové 41
🚊 Trams 1, 8, 25 and 26
Open: Mon–Fri 0730–1800,
Sat 0700–1100

Fish and poultry are the mainstays here: smoked mackerel, shellfish, roll mop herring, salmon fillets and roast chicken to name but a few.

Rytina 24

Strossmayerovo náměstí, corner of Dukelských hrdinů
🚇 Metro Vltavská; trams 1, 5, 8, 12, 17, 25 and 26
Open: Mon–Fri 0700–1900,
Sat 0700–1200

Large supermarket stocked up with cheeses, conserves, wines and old-fashioned fresh bread.

Letenské sady

Trams 12 and 17

A superb vantage point with panoramic views across the city, this sparsely wooded park is threaded with scenic paths well suited to picnicking. As well as specially designated picnic areas, there are kiosks selling alcohol and soft drinks in front of the **Letensky Zámeček** restaurant (*see page 61*). The Metronome sculpture was installed to commemorate the Velvet Revolution – a 30m-high statue of Stalin once occupied this strategic site. While you're in the vicinity, take a look at the charming neo-baroque gazebo, known as the **Hanavsky Pavilon**, now a café-restaurant (*see page 61*).

Stromovka

U Výstaviště

Trams 5, 12 and 17

The Royal Enclosure at Stromovka is one of the city's finest parks. Originally a hunting ground belonging to the kings of Bohemia, it was redesigned as an ornamental garden in 1593. Since the beginning of the 19th century Stromovka has been open to the public and it remains a popular recreation spot.

The main thoroughfare, known as Chestnut Avenue, leads to the formal gardens and passes the Rudolph II Water Tunnel – an aqueduct over 1000m long, built in 1584 to bring water from the River Vltava to feed the lakes. Continue through the woods to the top of a steep hill and you'll come to a medieval hunting lodge, converted in 1805 to a neo-Gothic summer residence (not open to the public). Fairs and exhibitions are still held on the Výstaviště, a site created specially for the 1891 Jubilee. Among the permanent attractions here are the Planetarium and the Lapidárium, a treasure trove of Czech sculptures dating from the 11th to 19th centuries – the exhibits include the original statues from the Charles Bridge.

▲ Letenské sady

Business restaurants

Dining in style

Prague is a regular venue on the international conference circuit and most of the leading hotels offer set business lunches or special menus.

- **Barock** *Pařížská 24, Celetná; ∅ 232 9221;* ⊚ *metro Staroměstská; open: daily 0830–0100; reservations recommended; all credit cards accepted; International-Asian;* ❷❷–❷❷❷. Relaxed informality is the trademark of this fashionable café-restaurant and cocktail bar, making it the perfect setting for closing deals or unwinding at the end of a trying day. Chill out on the terrace with Prague's beautiful people while feasting your eyes on the extensive list of Asian specials. Whether you order Thai, Chinese, Japanese or Korean, everything here rises to the occasion.
- **Café Patio** *Národní 22; ∅ 2491 8072;* ⊚ *trams 6, 9, 18, 21 and 22; open: Mon–Sat 1000–1900, Sun 1100–1900;* ❷❷. Fashionable café near the National Theatre, with a window on to one of Prague's most impressive art-nouveau avenues. There's an excellent choice of fresh salads (such as tuna or salmon) or pastries if you prefer.
- **Gourmet Club Restaurant and Lounge** *Hotel Palace, Panská 12, Celetná; ∅ 2409 3111;* ⊚ *metro Náměsti Republiky; open: daily 1200–2400; reservations essential; all credit cards accepted; International;* ❸❸❸. Modelled on an English gentlemen's club, this stylish restaurant should impress the most fastidious client. The genial *maitre d'hôte*, Mr Hudek, is on hand to advise on the menu before leaving you to take in the tasteful elegance of the surroundings and the mellifluous piano accompaniment.
- **U Kolowrata** *Valdštejnská 18, Nerudova; ∅ 531 546;* ⊚ *metro Malostranská; open: daily 1100–2300; reservations essential all credit cards accepted; Czech-International;* ❷❷–❷❷❷. The restaurant takes its name from the 18th-century owner of the house, the Count of Kolowrat. The special lunch menu, available from 1100 until 1700, has proved popular with both Czech and visiting businessmen who value the intimate setting and elegant surroundings. Game specialities include saddle of venison and wild duck breast in rose hip sauce.
- **Sarah Bernhardt Restaurant** *Hotel de Pařiž, Celetná; ∅ 2219 5811;* ⊚ *metro Náměsti Republiky; open: daily 0800–2300; reservations recommended; all credit cards accepted; French;* ❸❸❸. The Hotel Pařiž was designed in the early 1900s by Jan Vejrych and Antonín Pfeiffer. The restaurant, with its signature blue cleft mosaic, wooden wainscoting and

gilded stucco, is a superb example of art-nouveau décor and furnishings and the perfect setting for a relaxing meal. Business clients have included major corporations such as Hewlett Packard and Dupont, as well as the American Chamber of Commerce and the Czech Prime Minister, Vaclav Klaus. The cooking, by a Michelin-rated chef, is of the highest standard. Recommendations include *bouillabaisse*, veal fillets with cream of truffle and braised asparagus, and the crêpes Grand Marnier. Beaujolais and Burgundy feature prominently on the wine list, as well as Taittinger champagne.

> **The restaurant, with its signature blue cleft mosaic, wooden wainscoting and gilded stucco, is a superb example of art-nouveau décor.**

• **U Třech Modrých Koulí** *Havelská 8, Karlova; ✆ 2423 8130; Ⓜ metro Můstek; open: daily 1100–2300; reservations recommended; no credit cards accepted; International;* ❶❷. This charming house, known as the 'Three Blue Globes', dates from 1680. Mind your head as you descend the staircase to the cellar. The small dining spaces are the ideal environment for an informal working lunch. The menu is eclectic and includes tuna carpaccio, smoked salmon, steaks and beef stroganoff.

• **Triton** *Hotel Adria, Václavské náměstí 26, Wenceslas Square; ✆ 2108 1218; Ⓜ metro Můstek; open: daily 1200–2400; reservations essential; all credit cards accepted; International;* ❶❷❸. The décor of this hotel-restaurant with a prominent location on Wenceslas Square seizes the imagination. Descend from street level and you enter a spooky subterranean cavern, complete with stalactites, grottoes and reliefs depicting scenes from classical mythology. Once you've got over the setting, you'll be able to concentrate on the menu which includes fish and game specialities.

• **Zlatá Praha** *Hotel Intercontinental, Náměstí Curieových 43–5, Wenceslas Square; ✆ 2488 1111; Ⓜ tram 17; open: daily 1100–2300; reservations recommended; all credit cards accepted; Czech-International;* ❶❷❸. Located on the ninth (top) floor of Prague's most prestigious hotel, this formal restaurant offers superb views of the River Vltava, Prague Castle and the Lesser Town, along with food to satisfy the discriminating gourmand. There are half a dozen special business lunch menus (three and four courses) and an extensive à la carte list.

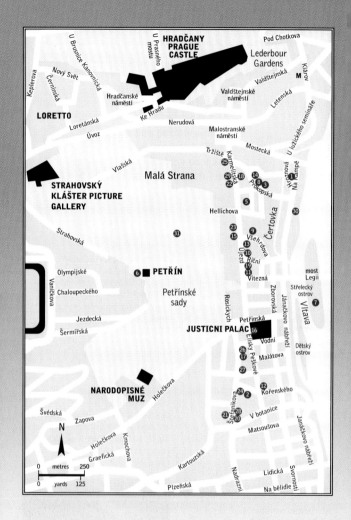

Petřín Park

The River Vltava is inevitably the focus of this part of the Lesser Town. Tables in the gardens and on the restaurant terraces overlooking the river are at a premium. You need only look to see why.

PETŘÍN PARK
Restaurants

Dvořák ❶

Na Kampě 3	
✆ 530 078	
🚋 Trams 12 and 22	
Open: daily 1030–2300	
Reservations recommended	
All credit cards accepted	
Czech	
❷❷	

At this hotel-restaurant in a lovely location on Kampa Island, the nicely presented Czech dishes include chicken steak with ginger, grilled pork with ham and asparagus and cold meat and cheese platters.

Fořtovna ❷

Arbesovo náměstí 1	
✆ 5732 0178	
🚋 Trams 6, 9 and 12	
Open: Mon–Sat 1000–2300	
Reservations unnecessary	
No credit cards accepted	
Czech	
❷❷	

This pleasantly unassuming neighbourhood restaurant specialises in traditional Bohemian cuisine, especially game. Dishes include stag and wild boar served up with generous helpings of Karlovy Vary dumplings. Pancakes with cranberries and whipped cream round off the meal nicely. Gambrinus draught beer is available, as well as a representative selection of Moravian wines.

Kampa Park ❶

Na Kampě 8	
✆ 5731 3493	
🚋 Trams 12 and 22	
Open: daily 1130–2300	
Reservations essential	
All credit cards accepted	
International	
❸❸❸	

The wonderful location on Kampa Island ensures that this Scandinavian-owned restaurant is never short of customers, despite the high prices and slightly aloof service. The sumptuous, candlelit interior is ideal for a romantic dinner but most visitors make a beeline for the riverside terrace and garden. While the meat dishes are appetising and inventive, the waterside setting will probably put you in the mood for pike, freshwater eel or one of the other fish specialities.

U Malířů ❸

Maltézské náměstí 11	
✆ 5732 0317	
🚋 Trams 12 and 22	
Open: daily 1130–2400	
Reservations essential	
All credit cards accepted	
French	
❸❸❸	

The house 'At the Painter's' dates from 1542 and, according to some accounts, was a

▲ Kampa Park

▲ U Malířů

hostelry almost from the word go. When the present restaurant opened nearly a decade ago, a bowl of soup cost the equivalent of an average worker's weekly wage and prices have remained off-puttingly high. What you pay for is cooking *sans pareil* and the authentic French ingredients flown in every day. The vaulted dining room is decorated with exquisite 17th-century frescos.

U Maltézských Rytířů 8

Prokopská 10

✆ 5753 3666
🚊 Trams 12 and 22
Open: daily 1100–2300
Reservations essential
All credit cards accepted
International
❷❷

Few of Prague's restaurants have such a deserved reputation for all-round consistency as the 'Knights of Malta'. Cosy and intimate, whether you're seated in the candlelit cellar or the tiny upstairs dining room, Madame Černikova will be on hand to ensure that your meal is an unforgettable one. Starters

include tomatoes stuffed with goats' cheese and served with sautéed green peppers. Game, poultry and fish all feature in the main courses – the roast venison with cranberry sauce and goose livers is out of this world. As for the desserts, the homemade apple strudel with ice cream and eggnog should be compulsory.

U Modré Kachničky 5

Nebovidska 6

✆ 5732 0308
🚊 Trams 12 and 22

Open: daily 1200–1600,
1830–2400

Reservations essential

No credit cards accepted

Czech

❷❷

'At the Blue Duckling'
consists of a maze of
tiny, beautifully
appointed dining rooms,
each of which is deco-
rated with paintings,
murals and engravings.
The Bohemian kitchen
features traditional
game dishes such as
venison cooked with
rose hip berries and hare
marinated in red wine.

Na Kampě 15

Na Kampě 15

✆ 5731 8996

🚃 Trams 12 and 22

Open: daily 1200–2400

Reservations recommended

All credit cards accepted

Czech-International

❷❷

In this cosy hotel-
restaurant with pub
terrace in a particularly
scenic corner of the
Lesser Town, the hearty
Czech fare includes tripe
soup, goulash, roast
goose breast and leg of
rabbit, all served with
lashings of dumplings,
potatoes and gravy.

Nebozízek

Petřínské sady 411

✆ 537 905

🚃 Trams 12 and 22 to
Újezd, then funicular to
Petřínské sady

Open: daily 1100–2300

Reservations recommended

All credit cards accepted

Czech

❷❷

Perched half way up
Petřín Hill, this popular
restaurant is reached by
funicular – getting there
is half the fun. The
panoramic views of
Prague from the terrace
are spectacular in fine
weather but the food
fails to impress.

Ostroff

Střelecký ostrov 336

✆ 2491 9235

🚃 Trams 6, 9 and 22

Open: Mon–Fri 1200–1400,
1900–2230, Sat 1900–
2230; cocktail bar daily
1200–0300

Reservations recommended

All credit cards accepted

Italian

❷❷❷

First pop upstairs to the
cocktail bar of this
trendy island eatery and
see if there's a table with
a view going spare. The
main dining space in the
spot-lit brick cellar lacks

atmosphere, although
the food can be heav-
enly, if expensive.

U Vladaře

Maltézké náměstí 10

✆ 5753 4121

🚃 Trams 12 and 22

Open: daily 1200–1500,
1800–2400

Reservations essential

All credit cards accepted

Czech

❷❷❷

This glamorous restau-
rant overlooking
Maltese Square has
attracted celebrities such
as Claudia Schiffer,
Gregory Peck and Miloš
Forman. The name
means 'At the
Sovereign' and the fine
old building dates from
1779. The décor
throughout is tasteful
and restrained, maybe a
little old-fashioned. The
Czech food (game and
fish specialities)
measures up to the most
discerning palate.

PETŘÍN PARK
Bars, cafés and pubs

Bar Bar ❾

Všehrdova 17

✆ 532 941

 Trams 12 and 22

Open: Mon–Fri 1100–2400,
Sat–Sun 1200–2400

€

Cellar bar decorated
with a themeless assort-
ment of bric-à-brac. The
salads and sweet and
savoury crêpes are
decidedly preferable to
the uninspired main
courses.

La Bastille ❿

Újezd 26

✆ 534 157

 Trams 12 and 22

Open: daily 1200–0100

€€

Gallic restaurant and
cocktail bar with
pronounced Czech lean-
ings. The brick décor
and mini-skirted wait-
resses makes for a
relaxed ambience. Sit
back and meander
through a menu which
ranges from French
onion soup or poultry
soup 'abounding with
vitamins' to honey duck
with apples, trout *à la
provençale* or kebabs
and chips.

Maltézské náměstí 9, 110 00 Praha 1
tel. 575 333 43

Bohemia Bagel ⓫

Újezd 16

✆ 530 921/0603 441434

Trams 12 and 22

Open: Mon–Fri 0700–2400,
Sat–Sun 0800–2400

€–€€

This cheerful, American-
style, self-service café is
a good place to
daydream or write your
postcards. The choice of
bagels is mind-boggling
– everything from apple
and cinnamon to
jalapeno, while the fill-
ings are out of this
world. Or you might be
tempted by the
brownies, club sand-
wiches, quiches or
veggie salads. The
multi-language menus
and takeaway service all
add to the offering.

Borzalino ⓬

Kořenského 12 (Arbesovo
náměstí)

✆ 5732 6048/0603 545827

Trams 6, 9 and 12

Open: daily 1100–2300

€€

Pizzas to takeaway or to
eat in, or you can have
them delivered to your
door via the **Food Taxi**
(✆ 2251 6732). Pasta
dishes are also available
and there's a good
selection of Italian
wines – Bardolino and
Montepulciano, as well
as Chianti and
Lambrusco.

Cantina ⓭

Újezd 38

✆ 5731 7173

Trams 12 and 22

Open: daily 1100–2400

€€

This bright and breezy
Tex-Mex serves cock-
tails alongside the stan-
dard menu of nachos,
fajitas, burritos and
quesadillas. Or you can
have a baked potato or
steak if you prefer.

El Centro ⓮

Maltézské náměstí 9

✆ 5753 3343

Trams 12 and 22

Open: daily 1100–0100

€€

This lively Spanish
bodega-bar on Maltese
Square offers a small
menu comprising salads,
pastas, omelettes and
grills. Brandy from Jerez
is a bit of a novelty in
Prague, Gambrinus beer,
less so.

U Černého Orla ⓯

Újezd 33

✆ None available

Trams 12 and 22

Open: Mon–Fri 1000–2200,
Sat–Sun 1100–2200

€€€

'At the Black Eagle' is a
traditional Prague

pivnice where you can buy a typical Czech pub lunch. Choose between roll mop herring, Hungarian sausages with mustard, salted herring, pork rolls and beer cheese with horse-radish, to name but a few delights. Staropramen and Plženský Prazdroj are available on draught and there's rum grog, mulled wine or tea and coffee if you prefer.

Diana

Náměstí Kinských 6
∅ 531 735
Trams 6, 9 and 12
Open: daily 1000–2400
●●

In this large, trendy snack bar and *vinárna*, the daily menu is commendably diverse, serving everything from traditional Czech soups (*kuřeci vyvar, Ceská veverka*) to Balkan cheese salad, goulash, spaghetti carbonara and Mexican dishes.

Einstein ⑰

Štefanikova 52
∅5732 2161
Trams 6, 9 and 12
Open: daily 1100–2300
No credit cards accepted
●●

On a street to the south of Petřín Park, this pizzeria also deals in pasta, gnocchi, mixed salads and novelty dishes including 'Albert's stuffed chicken steak' (Einstein, get it?). Krušovice beer on offer.

U Malého Glena ⑱

Karmelitská 23
∅ 535 8115
Trams 12 and 22
Open: daily 1000–0200
●●

An old-timer on the Lesser Town café circuit, 'Little Glen's' is a haven for English speaking ex-pats. Friendly and laid-back, you can drop in for a beer (Staropramen and Gambrinus on tap) or linger over a plate of warm pitta bread sand-wiches – the house speciality. The owner, Glen Spicer, is a jazz fan and hosts regular live concerts at the music club from 2100 onwards.

U Švejků ⑲

Újezd 22
∅ 535 629
Trams 6, 9 and 12
Open: daily 1100–2400
●●

Another pub cashing-in on the Švejk legend (*see page 26*), this place is a good lunchtime stop if you enjoy traditional Czech cooking at very reasonable prices, all washed down with a mug or two of Pilsner Urquell draught beer. The food is typical 'pub grub' with carp and potato salad on hand if you're not partial to meat. Carnivores have a field day with the likes of roast duck, smoked leg of pork and Peasant's Plate (including just about everything). An accor-dionist drops in from time to time.

PETŘÍN PARK
Shops, markets and picnic sites

Bakers

Cukrovinky ⑳

Štefanikova 28

🚋 Trams 6, 9 and 12

Open: Mon–Fri 0600–1800,
Sat 0800–1100

This confectioner's on
the road in from
Smíchov sells wines and
liqueurs, as well as cold
drinks and snacks.

Domácí Pečivo ㉑

Štefanikova 31

🚋 Trams 6, 9 and 12

Open: Mon–Fri 0700–1800,
Sat 0800–1200

This old-style local
bakery with tiled walls
also deals in basic
provisions including
wines and coffees.

Pekařství ㉒

Karmelitská 20

🚋 Trams 12 and 22

Open: Mon–Fri 0730–1845,
Sat–Sun 0900–1745

Inviting bakery with
café-bar – you can
smell the fresh bread as
you pass. Stop for a
coffee while choosing
from the enticing
displays of croissants,
strudels and ice creams.

Grocers

Bio Racio ㉓

Újezd 39/41

🚋 Trams 12 and 22

Open: Mon–Fri 0730–1800

Small grocer's with a
sideline in diet and
health foods.

Ovoce a Zelenina ㉔

Štefanikova 44

🚋 Trams 6, 9 and 12

Open: Mon–Fri 0700–1800,
Sat 0730–1200

Fruit and vegetable
shop also selling cartons
of fruit juice.

Potraviny ㉕

Karmelitská 25

🚋 Trams 12 and 22

Open: Mon–Sat 0700–2000

This grocery store offers
a large choice of Czech
beers and sparkling
wines.

Potraviny ❶

Na Kampě 6

🚋 Trams 12 and 22

Open: Mon–Sat 0700–2000,
Sun 0900–2000

Basically a wine shop,
but also dealing in fruit,
vegetables and essential
provisions.

Potraviny ㉖

Štefanikova 52, next to
Einstein (see page 73)

🚋 Trams 6, 9 and 12

Open: 24 hrs a day

On sale are souvenirs,
chocolates and a small
selection of groceries.

Potraviny u
Arbesa ㉗

Arbesovo náměstí/corner of
Štefanikova

🚋 Trams 6, 9 and 12

Open: Mon–Fri 0700–1830,
Sat 0700–1130

Large supermarket with
delicatessen counters
selling fresh fruit and
vegetables and bread.
You can also buy hot
snacks at the rotisserie,
plus a range of Czech
and international wines
and spirits, including
Jameson whiskey.

Potraviny Večerka 28

Štefanikova 28

🚊 Trams 6, 9 and 12

Open: Mon–Fri 0600–2100,
Sat–Sun 1000–2100

Mini-market selling filled rolls, as well as wines, spirits and soft drinks.

Wines

Obchůdek U Zlaté Koruny 29

Karmelitská 21

🚊 Trams 12 and 22

Open: daily 1100–1800

'The Golden Crown' offers a wide selection of Moravian wines (Rulandské Bílé, Modré Portugal, Zweigelt and so on), plus clarets, spirits and liqueurs. The displays of Bohemian glass are also worth a look.

Picnic sites

Na Kampě 30

🚊 Trams 12 and 22

Separating picturesque Kampa Island from the rest of the Lesser Town is the millstream known as Čertovka – the 'Devil's Stream'. Near the still-churning waterwheel of the Old Priory Mill, you'll find a couple of cafés with garden terraces overlooking the River Vltava – an idyllic spot if you get there before the crowds. The adjoining park is well suited to picnics.

▲ Petřín Park

Nearby:

Červena Sedma 1

Na Kampě 5

🚊 Trams 12 and 22

Open: daily 1100–2300

🌑–🌑🌑

Café selling vegetarian meals and snacks such as cheeses and plates of smoked meat. Staropramen and Gambrinus beers are on tap.

Petřín Park 31

Entrances on Újezd, Úvoz and Vlašská

🚊 Trams 12 and 22; funicular from Újezd

This beautiful hillside park offers superb views of the towers and spires of the Old Town. The lower slopes were planted with vineyards in the 12th century which were later replaced with orchards – when the apple and pear trees blossom in the spring it's a sight to behold. At the lower end of the park are the English-style **Kinský Gardens**, laid out in 1827. Skirting Petřín is the **Hunger Wall**, part of the city's defences built in the reign of Charles IV by peasants grateful for employment during a time of famine. You may also find time to visit the baroque church of St Lawrence.

The dominant landmark is the **Observation Tower**, a 60m-high replica of the Eiffel Tower, erected for the Prague Jubilee celebrations in 1891. The labyrinthine **Mirror Maze**, with a diorama of the Defence of Prague against the Swedes as its focal point, dates from the same period. To get to the top of the hill without too much exertion, take the funicular from Újezd. Half way up you'll notice the **Nebozízek** terrace restaurant (*see page 71*).

Breakfast and brunch

Stoking up for the day

American ex-pats deserve most of the credit for the revolution in breakfast eating in Prague. Nowadays you can choose the kind of meal you want to start the day while Sunday brunch is a treat.

• **Avalon Bar and Grill** *Malostranské náměstí 12, Nerudova;* ✆ *530 276;* 🚊 *trams 12 and 22; open: daily 1100–2400; brunch Sat–Sun 1100–1800;* ❶❷-❶❷❸. This popular American hangout on Lesser Town Square wins friends all the time with its extensive menu and cool, casual style. Brunch is a set-price, three-course affair with as many non-alcoholic drinks as you want. You can also order salads, club sandwiches or fudge sundaes.

• **Bellevue** *Smetanovo nábřeží 18, New Town;* ✆ *5732 0570;* 🚊 *trams 17 and 18; open: daily; reservations essential;* ❶❷. So-called because of the views of the River Vltava from the terrace. On weekdays you can order from the buffet (eat as much as you can) or à la carte. Sunday brunch is served up with live or recorded jazz. Other plusses are freshly

squeezed orange juice and chilled bottles of Bohemia Sekt.

• **Break Café Deli** *Stepanská 32, Národní Třída;* ✆ *2223 1065;* 🚊 *metro Národní Třída; open: Mon–Sat 0730–2300; no credit cards accepted;* ❶❷. Continental breakfasts are served daily in this popular New Town rendezvous.

• **Le Café Colonial** *Široká 6, Celetná;* ✆ *2481 8322;* 🚊 *metro Staroměstská; open: breakfast 0900–1100, then 1000–2400;* ❶-❶❷. Popular Josefov café with bright, multi-coloured walls and exotic North African and Asian ornaments. For breakfast, order a cappuccino, then visit the bakery and sample the genuine French croissants and baguettes.

• **Cornucopia Sports Café** *Jungmannova 10, Wenceslas Square;* ✆ *2422 0950;* 🚊 *metro Müstek; open: Mon–Fri 0730–2200, Sat 0930–2000, Sun 1000–1600;* ❶-❶❷. A mainly expatriate crowd comes here on weekdays to watch CNN news while tucking into toasted muffins or ham, eggs and chips. The seven-option Sunday brunch is popular with armchair sports fans so arrive early if you want a seat. On the menu are French toast with chocolate and walnut, eggs (cooked any way you want), potatoes, beans and burritos.

• **Grand Restaurant Septim** *Rašínovo nábřeží 59, New Town;* ✆ *298 559;* 🚊 *trams 17 and 21; open: daily 0930–2400;* ❶❷. This

▲ Relaxing in the Old Town

New Town eatery, near the Palacký Bridge, has started offering brunch at weekends.

- **James Joyce** *Liliová 10, Karlova; ✆ 2424 8793; Ⓜ metro Staroměstská; open: daily 1030– 0100;* ❷❷. Full Irish breakfast – bacon, sausages, eggs, beans.
- **O'Ché's** *Liliová 16, Karlova; ✆ 2222 1178; Ⓜ metro Staroměstská; open: 1000–2400 (kitchen 1000– 2200);* ❶–❷❷. Crazily-named Irish pub where, apart from the usual draught Guinness and Kilkenny you can order a full English breakfast (bacon, eggs, tomatoes available 1000–1800) or a vegetarian alternative.
- **Oscar's** *Tynsky dvůr 1, Celetná; Ⓜ metro Náměstí Republiky; ✆ 2489 5404;* ❸❸❸. Tucked away in the picturesque Týn courtyard, Oscar's rustles up an American-style brunch available at weekends (1000– 1600) at a good price.
- **Pálffy Palác Club** *Valdštejnská 14, Nerudova; ✆ 513 2418; Ⓜ metro Malostranská; open: daily 1100– 2300; fixed price lunch Mon–Fri 1100–1700; brunch Sat–Sun 1100–1500; all credit cards accepted;* ❸❸❸. The weekend brunch (served 1100 to 1500) in this stately baroque palace below Hradčany is one of the best in Prague. The choice includes fresh croissants, omelettes, chocolate muesli with fresh fruits and yoghurt, grilled duck breast on curry, honey and oranges, and roasted quails with apricot sauce.

▲ V Zátíší restaurant

- **Thirsty Dog** *Elišky Krásnohorské 5; ✆ 231 0039; open: daily 1200–0200;* ❷❷. Sunday brunch is served in a shady courtyard to the mellow strains of jazz – very cool and relaxing. A variety of 'fantasy' breakfasts is also available, for example '*quesadilla* San Miguel' (chicken breasts with avocado and a cheese and egg omelette), 'Shepherd's' (pork chop topped with apple butter) and French toast stuffed with banana, cream and ice cream. Other restaurants that serve a good brunch at weekends are:
- **Café Louvre:** excellent choice of breakfasts: Cowboy, French English, American, German (*see page 32*).
- **J J Murphys & Co:** Irish-style brunch at weekends (*see page 54*).
- **Red Hot & Blues:** Mexican-style brunch with creole dishes (*see page 11*).
- **U 14 Pomocníků:** the choice includes yoghurt and muesli, cereals, vegetable salads and ham and eggs (*see page 83*).
- **V Zátíší:** classic brunch even includes roast beef (*see page 21*).

> **Chocolate muesli with fresh fruits and yoghurt, grilled duck breast on curry, honey and oranges, and roasted quails with apricot sauce.**

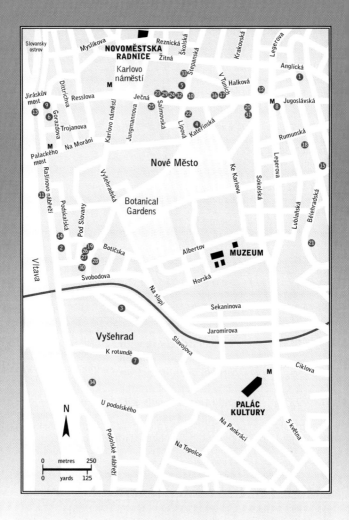

New Town and Vyšehrad

The New Town was actually founded in the 15th century. Eateries cluster around Charles Square (Prague's largest) and along the embankment. Most visitors go on to explore the ancient citadel of Vyšehrad – a good picnic spot with wonderful views.

NEW TOWN AND VYŠEHRAD
Restaurants

Baretta ❶

| Bělehradská 4 |
| Ø 6121 5622 |
| 🚊 Trams 6 and 11 |
| Open: Mon–Sat 1030–2200, Sun 1700–2200 |
| Reservations recommended |
| No credit cards accepted |
| Italian |
| 🟢🟢 |

Zany décor gives this New Town pizzeria the edge over its rivals. The pizzas aren't bad either and there are plenty of toppings to choose from, along with pasta dishes and other Italian standards.

Le Bistrot de Marlène ❷

| Plavecka 4 |
| Ø 291 077 |
| 🚊 Trams 17 and 21 |
| Open: Mon–Fri 1200–1430, 1900–2230, Sat 1900–2230 |
| Reservations essential |
| All credit cards accepted |
| French |
| 🟢🟢🟢 |

Marlène Salomon's cosy bistro has been a jewel in Prague's culinary crown for some years now and standards have remained high. That said, starters and salads tend to outshine the main courses, while too many patrons seem out to impress. Two candlelit dining rooms suggest warmth, romance and the rural idyll. Try *foie gras de canard* or *poêlée calamari frits à la provençal.*

Dolly Bell ❸

| Neklanova 20 |
| Ø 298 815 |
| 🚊 Trams 3, 16, 17 and 21 |
| Open: daily 1400–2400 |
| Reservations recommended |
| 💳 American Express |
| Balkan-Mediterranean |
| 🟢🟢 |

This Yugoslav restaurant has made something of a name for itself in recent years. The wholesome, homely Balkan cooking features *burek* (tasty meat and potato pastries), kebabs, moussaka and Begova soup. Leave room for desserts, especially *tufahija* (baked apple filled with nuts and whipped cream). The surreal décor – tables suspended from the ceiling – helps to give the place a fun feel.

JB Club Restaurant ❹

| Kateřinská 7 |
| Ø 2491 8425 |
| Ⓜ Metro I P Pavlova |
| Open: Mon–Fri 1200–2400, Sat 1700–2400 |
| Reservations recommended |
| 💳 💳 💳 |
| International |
| 🟢🟢 |

Steaks are the stock-in-trade of this pleasant, if somewhat staid, diner near St Katherine's Church. You are welcomed by courteous staff.

▲ Na Rybárně

U Ječmene ⑤

Stepanská 2

∅ None available

🚋 Trams 4, 6, 16, 22 and 34

Open: daily 1100–0100

Reservations unnecessary

No credit cards accepted

Czech

❷❸

This old-fashioned Czech restaurant, not far from Wenceslas Square, has a menu featuring schnitzel and other traditional Bohemian mainstays. A lunch menu is available from 1100 until 1500.

Na Rybárně ⑥

Gorazdova 17

∅ 299 795

🚇 Metro Karlovo náměstí

Open: Mon–Sat, 1200–2400, Sun 1700–2400

Reservations recommended

No credit cards accepted

Czech

❷❸

This unassuming fish restaurant was a favourite of Václav Havel's in the days before he became president. The menu (available in English) has livened up a good deal since those trying times and features the likes of shrimp soup, trout cooked in wine with an envelope of cabbage leaves and a satisfyingly tangy pike-perch with chilli seasoning.

Na Vyšehradě ⑦

K rotundě 2

∅ 2423 9297

🚇 Metro Vyšehrad

Open: daily 1000–2300

Reservations recommended

No credit cards accepted

Czech

❷❸

At the heart of the ancient hilltop citadel of Vyšehrad, this unpretentious eatery is a convenient lunch stop if you're giving the local sights the once over. Comfortable and relaxing with a typical range of Czech dishes on the menu.

Peking ⑧

Legerova 64, corner of Náměstí I P Pavlova

∅ 293 531

🚇 Metro I P Pavlova

Open: daily 1130–2300

Reservations unnecessary

All credit cards accepted

Chinese

❷❸

Don't be put off by the appearance of this dour, weathered building just a few steps from the entrance to the metro station. The interior is much more inviting, while the typical meat and seafood dishes have more of a kick than is usual in this part of Europe. Takeaway delivery service by **Food Taxi** (∅ 2251 6732).

La Perle de Prague ⑨

Tančící Dům, Rašínovo nábřeží 80 by Jiráskův Bridge

∅ 2198 4160

🚋 Trams 3, 17 and 21

Open: Tue–Fri 1200–1400, 1930–2230, Mon 1930–2230

Reservations recommended

All credit cards accepted

French

❷❸❹

This gourmand temple, located on the seventh floor of the 'Dancing House' (a fascinating, avant-garde building which seems to collapse in on itself), is celebrated for its panoramic views of the city – you can wander on to the rooftop terrace at the end of your meal if you wish. The gastronomic delights include morels with homemade toast, breast of duck cooked in a rich port wine sauce, roasted salmon with spinach, and sea bass (fish lovers are in for a treat here as the shellfish is also excellent). The business lunch is good value.

U Šumavy

Stepanská 3

Ø 292 0051

🚊 Trams 4, 6, 16, 22 and 34

Open: daily 1100–2300

Reservations unnecessary

No credit cards accepted

Czech

❷❸

Look out for a large cream building opposite St Stephen's Church. It serves standard Bohemian fare: goulash, pork roulade and meat dumplings. Budvar lager is available on draught.

Vltava ⓫

Quay below Rašínovo nábřeží, by Palackého Bridge

Ø 294 964

🚊 Trams 17 and 21

Open: daily 1100–2200

Reservations recommended

No credit cards accepted

Czech

❷❸

Just a few steps from the River Vltava, this fish restaurant makes the most of a lovely riverside setting. The grilled trout and the fish

soup can be recommended. Outdoor seating.

Z Kamene ⓬

Sokolská 60

Ø None available

🚇 Metro I P Pavlova

Open: Mon–Sat 1100–0100, Sun 1100–2300; *vinárna* Mon–Fri 1800–0100

Reservations unnecessary

No credit cards accepted

Czech-International

❷❸

In this friendly neighbourhood restaurant on a busy road, the eclectic menu includes beefsteak, trout 'in the miller's style', Szechuan pork and chicken Kung-Pao (incredibly popular in Prague for some reason). English breakfasts are also on offer.

▲ Frieze in Na Rybárně

NEW TOWN AND VYŠEHRAD
Bars, cafés and pubs

U Hastrmana 🔞

Quay below Rašínovo
nábřeži, by Jiráskův Bridge

Ø 299 344

🚋 Trams 17 and 21

Open: daily 1100–0100

💶💶

Good-value fish restaurant, hidden from view by the embankment.

U Libuše 🔢

Plavecká corner of
Podskalská

Ø None available

🚋 Trams 17 and 21

Open: Mon–Fri 0930–2300,
Sat–Sun 1030–2300

💶💶

'Spit-and-sawdust' Prague pub with a restaurant to the rear. Classic Czech dishes

such as beefsteak with egg, schnitzel and roast chicken adorn the menu. Staropramen draught lager is the tipple.

Merlin 🔢

Bělehradská 68a

Ø 2252 2054

🚋 Trams 6 and 11

Open: Mon–Fri 1130–2400,
Sat–Sun 1500–2400

💶💶

On the edge of the New Town, Merlin can loosely be described as an Irish bar with Czech input. The food is a mixed bag of Czech, Mexican and Italian dishes, some of which don't come off. Try the *moules provençales* on aubergine and tomato salad, the *fajitas* and

the Czech meat dishes. Service is a little slow.

U Mlsného Bobra 🔢

Ječná 41–3

Ø None available

🚋 Trams 4, 6, 16, 22 and 34

Open: daily 0900–2200

💶💶

This express pizzeria is part of the Alfredo chain. Other dishes include risotto, lasagne, fillet of fish or nachos. The confectionery counter sells pizza slices as well as cakes and pastries.

U Pádivce 🔢

Ječná 41–3

Ø None available

▲ Vegetarian brunch at Radost FX Café

@ Trams 4, 6, 16, 22 and 34

Open: Mon–Fri 1000–2200, Sat–Sun 1300–2100

©

Tiny wine bar and shop (wine sold by the glass or bottle). Moravian wines include Müller-Thurgau, Veltinské Zelené and Vavřinecké.

U Pastýřky ⑱

Bělehradská 15

✆ 434 093

@ Trams 6 and 11

Open: daily 1800–0100

All credit cards accepted

©©

Finally the Slovaks get a look-in! The log cabin décor and wood-fired grill make for a homely ambience while you tuck into your steak.

U Pěti Králů ⑲

Vyšehradská 9

✆ None available

@ Trams 7, 18 and 24

Open: Mon–Fri 1100–2230, Sun 1100–2200

©–©©

'The Five Kings' is a smoky pub-restaurant specialising in pasta dishes, gnocchi, steaks and salads. Staropramen beer is on tap.

Pizza Go Home ⑳

Sokolská 31

✆ None available

@ Metro I P Pavlova

Open: daily 1100–2400

©

Takeaway pizza place, near the Hotel Legie, which also sells chicken salads.

Radost FX Café ㉑

Bělehradská 120

✆ 2425 4776

@ Trams 6 and 11

Open: daily 1130–0400

No credit cards accepted

©–©©

At last a place for vegetarians! This trendy café has been around for long enough to attract a loyal clientele. Late-night opening and weekend brunch are the other recommendations.

Restaurace Pivovarský Dům ㉒

Lipová 15

✆ 9621 6666

@ Trams 4, 6, 16, 22 and 34

Open: daily 1100–2330

No credit cards accepted

©©

The 'Beerhouse' offers up-and-coming, as well as traditional, beers. The food is nothing special but it's cheap and includes goulash, and beef sirloin in cream sauce.

Svět ㉓

Ječná 5

✆ 2492 0509

@ Trams 4, 6, 16, 22 and 34

Open: daily 0800–2230

©©

A high-street café with plastic seating and eclectic menu – soups, baguettes, Mexican cutlets, calamari, salmon carpaccio, potatoes 'los tornados', peppered steak, and so on. Draught beers

Ječná 15
120 00 Praha 2

include Guinness and Staropramen.

U 14 Pomocníků ㉔

Ječná 15

✆ 9621 2015

@ Trams 4, 6, 16, 22 and 34

Open: Mon–Fri 0800–2300, Sat–Sun 1030–2300

©©

The yellow banner strung across the street ensures that you can't miss this lively café-bar. If you've missed your hotel breakfast you can catch up here. The choice includes yoghurt and muesli, cereals, vegetable salads and ham and eggs. Lunch dishes include pizzas and steaks.

V Ječně ㉕

Ječná 4

✆ None available

@ Trams 4, 6, 16, 22 and 34

Open: daily 0900–2300

©

Old-fashioned snack bar offering daily specials and Staropramen on draught.

NEW TOWN AND VYŠEHRAD
Shops, markets and picnic sites

Bakers and confectioners

Cukrárna D & D 26

Vyšehradská 11

Ⓜ Trams 7, 18 and 24

Open: daily 0900–1900

Confectionery shop selling the usual range of sweets, chocolates and ice creams.

Pekařství 27

Vyšehradská 11

Ⓜ Trams 7, 18 and 24

Open: Mon–Fri 0700–1830, Sat 0700–1200

Small local bakery.

Grocers and supermarkets

Lahůdky 28

Vyšehradská 6

Ⓜ Trams 7, 18 and 24

Open: daily 0600–1800

Grocery store with a large delicatessen counter, selling drinks and other provisions.

Obchod čerstvých uzenín 29

Ječná 13

Ⓜ Trams 4, 6, 16, 22 and 34

Open: Mon–Fri 0700–1800

Neighbourhood butcher's shop where you can buy cooked meats and also bread, soft drinks and ice cream.

Ovoce a zelenina Vyšehrad 30

Vyšehradská 13

Ⓜ Trams 7, 18 and 24

Open: Mon–Fri 0800–1830, Sat 0800–1200

Fruit and vegetable shop with a large fridge for alcoholic and soft drinks.

Potraviny 31

Sokolská 29

Ⓜ Metro I P Pavlova

Open: Mon–Fri 0800–1900, Sat 0800–1200

Corner grocery shop selling fresh fruit and vegetables, also cakes, beers and spirits.

Řeznictví 32

Stepanská 1

Ⓜ Trams 3, 9, 14 and 21

Open: Mon–Sat 0730–1400

Butcher's shop with a large deli counter displaying a selection of cooked meats. The rotisserie sells grilled chicken, goulash and other hot snacks – you can eat in (standing room only) or takeaway.

Rychlé Občerstvení 33

Stepanská 39a

Ⓜ Trams 4, 6, 16, 22 and 34

Open: daily 0800–2000

Stand-up snack bar doling out fast food.

Picnic sites

Vyšehrad 34

Ⓜ Metro Vyšehrad

According to legend it was on this rocky headland, on the right bank of the River Vltava, that Princess Libuše experienced a vision of a glorious city. After marrying the ploughman, Přemysl, the pair went on to found the Přemyslid dynasty which ruled Bohemia for more than 800 years. The strategic importance of Vyšehrad was recognised long before Hradčany. In the 11th century, King Vratislav II made Vyšehrad his official residence and built a fortified palace on the site. It was more than a hundred years before the kings and princes of Bohemia finally abandoned Vyšehrad for Prague Castle.

Today Vyšehrad is a kind of miniature Czech theme park. A marked trail guides visitors around the extensive landscaped garden and its most important sights –the information office has a useful leaflet. The focal point of the former citadel is the Church of St Peter and St Paul, rebuilt in the 19th century – the neo-Gothic spires are as much a landmark as St Vitus' Cathedral. On the lawn near the church is a medieval well, with groups of statues by the 19th-century sculptor, Josef Myslbek, which were removed from the Palacký Bridge in 1945. You can picnic on the ruined fortifications, taking in the views from the terrace. Vyšehrad cemetery is Prague's Père Lachaise – among the distinguished artists and intellectuals buried here are the composers, Antonín Dvořák and Bedřich Smetana, the painter Alfons Mucha and the writer, Karel Čapek. The elaborate entrance to the citadel, the Leopold Gate, dates from 1670. Predating it by some six hundred years is St Martin's Rotunda, one of the earliest Christian buildings in Bohemia.

If you want to supplement your picnic, the restaurant **Na Vyšehradě** (*see page 80*) can be found on K rotundě, the road which leads through the centre of the fortifications.

▲ Picnicking at St Peter and St Paul

International restaurants

If you've had enough Czech game …

The growth of international dining over the last 10 years has been little short of astonishing and represents increasingly diverse culinary cultures developing in Prague.

- **Casablanca** *Na příkopě 10, Národní Třída;* ✆ *2421 0519;* ⓜ *metro Můstek; open: daily 1800–2430; summer terrace 1200–0030; reservations recommended; all credit cards accepted; Moroccan;* ❶❷❸. You'll find the Casablanca in the building known as the Savarin Palace. No effort has been spared to transport you from Europe to the shores of North Africa – attentive staff dressed in loose-fitting robes, silver tableware, colourful brocades and cushions and the obligatory belly dancer.

- **Chez Moi** *Tomášská 12, Nerudova;* ✆ *539 783;* ⓜ *trams 12 and 22; open: daily 1200–2400; reservations recommended; all credit cards accepted; French-International;* ❶❷. Located in a secluded corner of the Lesser Town, Chez Moi is an informal cellar eatery with a romantic candlelit ambience. If you wish, you can eat outdoors on the garden terrace. The accent is on Provençal cooking and you can order French, as well as Czech, wines from the premier vineyards of Žernosek and Mikulov.

- **Fakhreldine** *Stepanská 32, Národní Třída;* ✆ *2223 2617;* ⓜ *metro Můstek; open: Mon–Sat 1100–2400; reservations essential; all credit cards accepted; Lebanese;* ❶❷❸. Dinner doesn't come cheap here, but Fakhreldine is rated one of the finest Lebanese restaurants this side of Beirut. Once you've ordered some of the mouth-watering fresh bread, make a beeline for the *meze*: houmous, *tabouleh*, *labneh* (cream cheese), vine leaves stuffed with rice and vegetables, the list goes on and on. If you order half a dozen of these appetisers you could pass on the main course and save yourself some money. Otherwise the pick of the lamb specialities is probably the minced meat *kafta khashkash*, cooked with parsley and garlic and served with a tangy tomato sauce.

- **Kebab House** *Perlová 1, Karlova;* ✆ *0603 317158;* ⓜ *metro Můstek; open: daily 1100–2200; reservations unnecessary; no credit cards accepted; Turkish;* ❶❷. Turkish restaurants are thin on the ground in Prague – this one is near Wenceslas Square. The menu includes doner and Iskender kebabs and *börek* (rich layered cheese pastry).

- **Modrá Řeka** *Mánesova 13, Wenceslas Square;* ✆ *2225 1601;*

▲ Russian Samovar

tram 11; open: Mon–Fri 1100–2300, Sat–Sun 1300–2300; reservations recommended; no credit cards accepted; Balkan-Yugoslavian; ❷❸. A little off the beaten track, this old Prague favourite takes its name, Blue River, from a popular Balkan rock song of the 1980s. Small and homely, it offers traditional south Slav cooking in large portions and at knockdown prices. Typical dishes include *čevapčiči* (rissoles served with *kajmak*, a delicious salted clotted cream), *gibanica* (curd cheese pie), *dolma* platter (green peppers and onions, stuffed with lamb, rice and peppers and wrapped in vine leaves).

• **Russian Samovar** *Dittrichova 25, Národní Třída; ✆ 299 011;* ⓜ *metro Karlovo náměstí; open: daily 1200–2400; reservations recommended; all credit cards accepted; Russian;* ❶❷❸. Folksy gourmet restaurant favoured by wealthy business types. The cost soon mounts up if you follow Russian tradition and order several hors d'oeuvres. Caviar is the speciality of the house (served with eggs and blinis) and the sturgeon and smoked salmon are also first rate. *Solyanka* (a thick, meaty soup) is almost a meal in itself but you should leave room for the *shashlik* of Peter the Great (skewered lamb with kidneys, marinated in yoghurt).

• **Le Saint Jacques** *Jakubská 4, Celetná; ✆ 232 2685;* ⓜ *metro Náměstí Republiky; open: Mon–Fri 1200–1500, 1800–2400, Sat*

1800–2400; reservations recommended; all credit cards accepted; French; ❷❸. The candlelit interior of this family-run restaurant, named after the nearby Franciscan church, suggests romantic dining, though couples seated near the plate-glass window may not relish the curious stares of passers-by. Scallops (*coquilles St-Jacques*) is the speciality of the house and worth serious consideration, otherwise, try the melt-in-your-mouth quiche Lorraine.

No effort has been spared to transport you from Europe to the shores of North Africa.

• **Taj Mahal** *Škretova 10, Národní Třída; ✆ 2422 5566;* ⓜ *trams 6 and 11; open: Mon–Sat 1200–2330, Sun 1500–2300; reservations recommended; American Express* 🟦 💳; *Indian;* ❷❸. Authentic Indian restaurant with a welcoming ambience, unobtrusive décor and tasty mainstream dishes such as chicken tikka biriyani, prawn tandoori and lamb passanda (slices of lamb fillet, marinated in spices and yoghurt, then cooked with herbs in curry).

Food etiquette and culture

Eating out in Prague is more enjoyable than ever. There are literally hundreds of good-value restaurants pandering to every conceivable customer and palate. Equally good news for visitors is that the choice of cuisines is also growing all the time – newcomers on the scene include Australian, Lebanese, Jewish and Thai. Standards of service are improving and, while culinary finesse and expertise still fall short of Parisian standards, it is definitely on the up, thanks to a new generation of enthusiastic young chefs, many of whom have trained abroad.

WHERE TO EAT

The old distinction between a *restaurace* and a **vinárna** is fast becoming meaningless, at least as far as tourists are concerned. Broadly speaking, a *vinárna* is a restaurant where wine is served – a wine bar you might say, or, as is more often the case, a wine cellar. A **restaurace** tends to be more formal and expensive, though a better guide to price is the rating (*skupina I, II, III, IV*) advertised on the door. Only first-rate establishments merit *skupina I*, while most fall into the second category. Nearly all of Prague's restaurants enjoy stunning locations – a converted water mill, a baroque palace, a Gothic cellar, a rooftop terrace with panoramic views … you can take your pick.

If you're happier with informal bonhomie and plain home cooking, head for the local pub or **tavern** (*hospoda, hostinec, pivnice*). *(See page 36 for more details.)*

A vibrant **café culture** is fast emerging, while the traditional *kavárna* is constantly reinventing itself. Rubbing shoulders with famous names such as the Slavia, the Europa and the Café de Paris, are feisty newcomers with a penchant for garish colour schemes, provocative décor, disco music and novelty menus.

If you're too busy sightseeing to linger over a meal, call in at a **pastry shop** (*cukrárna*) for cream cakes, sandwiches and pizza

▲ Café de Paris

slices, or a **delicatessen** (*lahůdky*) as many are equipped with a rotisserie. Finally, there's the **fast food stall** (*občerstvení*) where you can pick up a burger, frankfurter, hot dog, corn on the cob and other snacks.

SMOKING AND VEGETARIANS

As yet, relatively few restaurants have specially designated non-smoking areas. The situation is not much better for vegetarians; while almost every menu will contain at least one vegetarian item, this will often be no more substantial or imaginative than mushroom omelette or grilled cheese on toast. Remember too that even soups without meat are often made using meat stock. The best advice is to declare yourself at the outset by saying, '*Jsem vegetarian[ka]*' (I am a vegetarian), or '*maso nejím*' (I don't eat meat).

WHEN TO EAT

While an increasing number of restaurants stay open until the early hours of the morning, many kitchens close at around 2230. Lunch (*oběd*) in restaurants is served from around midday until approximately 1500, but more informal eateries serve throughout the day. Continental, American and British breakfasts (*snídaně*) are increasingly available, as is brunch at weekends. Most Czechs dine early (from around 1800). Finding a table *somewhere* isn't a problem, but if you want a choice in the matter, **be sure to book** – if you see somewhere you like the look of during the day, reserve a table for the evening.

HOW TO ORDER

The typical Czech menu (*Jídelní lístek*) is divided into: cold dishes (*studená jídla*), hot starters (*teplé předkrmy*), soups (*polévky*), fish (*ryby*), poultry (*drůbež*), and main courses (*hotová jídla*). Most places offer a fixed price dish or menu of the day (*nabídka dne*) which is often excellent value. Main courses generally arrive with generous side servings of potatoes, dumplings or rice, as well as vegetables of some description. If you want a salad, you should order it separately.

Standards of **service** have greatly improved in recent years but you should still watch out for sharp practice. Insist on a formal itemised bill. There will usually be a small cover charge as well as VAT; a service charge may also be included. **Tipping** is at your discretion (10 per cent is more than acceptable) – remember that it's the custom to hand the waiter the money rather than leave it behind on the table. If you're paying by credit card, write out all sums in full to avoid subsequent fraud.

Menu decoder

COOKING METHODS
grilovaný – grilled
pečený – roasted
smažený – fried
uzený – smoked
vařený – boiled, cooked

CONDIMENTS
hořčice – mustard
majonéza – mayonnaise
ocet – vinegar
olivový olej – olive oil
omáčka – sauce
pepř – pepper
smetana – cream
sůl – salt

BREADS
chléb – bread
chlebíček – sandwich
pletená houska – knotted roll
rohlík – finger roll
zitný chléb – rye bread

PŘEDKRMY (APPETISERS)
bryndza – goats' cheese in brine
humrový salát s majonézou – lobster salad with mayonnaise

omeleta s hráškem – green pea omelette
paštika – pâté, usually served with gherkins
plněná šunka – rolls of ham stuffed with whipped cream and coarsely grated horseradish
pražská šunka s křenem – Prague ham
rajčata plněná krabím masem – tomatoes stuffed with crab meat
rajčata plněná zeleninou a sýrem – tomatoes stuffed with vegetables and cheese
ruské vejce a majonézou – egg with mayonnaise
smažený sýr – slices of Edam fried in batter or au gratin
tvaroh s ředkvičkami – cream cheese with radishes
uzený losos – smoked salmon
vepřový rosol s jablkovým křenem – smoked pigs' tongue with apple and horseradish
žampióny s vejci – mushrooms with eggs

POLÉVKY (SOUPS)
bramborová polévka s houbami – potato and mushroom soup
chřestová – asparagus soup
čočková – lentil soup
dršťková – tripe soup
fazolová – green bean soup
gulášová polévka – spicy goulash soup
hnědá (hovězí) – consommé
houbová – mushroom soup
hovězí polévka s játrovými

knedličky – liver dumplings in beef broth
hrachová – pea soup
kulajda – vegetable soup
nudlová – noodle soup
rajčatova polévka – tomato soup
slepicý – chicken soup
zeleninová – vegetable soup

HOTOVÁ JÍDLA/JÍDLA NA MINUTKY (MAIN COURSES)

These are often divided on menus into dishes ready to be served and to order (*à la minute*).

MEAT (MASO), POULTRY (DRŮBEZ) AND GAME (ZVEŘINA)

bažant – pheasant
hovězí – beef
  biftek s vejcem – beefsteak with a fried egg
  hovězí vařené – boiled beef
  hovězí guláš – beef goulash, a spicy rich stew originating in Hungary
  pražská hovězí pečeně – joint of Prague roast beef stuffed with fried diced ham, peas, egg, onions and spices
  roštěnka s rýží – stewed steak with rice
  smažený vepřový řízek – pork schnitzed served perhaps with potato salad
  svíčková na smetaně – beef sirloin served in a creamy vegetable sauce
husa – goose
  pečená husa (kachna) – roast goose (duck)
játra – liver
  anglická játra – liver *à l'anglaise*
jazyk – tongue
jehněčí – lamb
jitrnice – black pudding

kachna – duck
kanec – boar
klobása – sausage (*párky* are frankfurters)
kotlety zapečené v sýru – cutlets fried in cheese
králík – rabbit
krůta – turkey
kuře – chicken
  kuře na rožni – grilled chicken
lečo – Hungarian ratatouille
ledvinky – kidneys
skopové – mutton
srnčí – venison
telecí – veal
  přírodní telecí řízek s brambory/rýží – slice of veal with potatoes and rice
  telecí – slices of veal, prepared with paprika, rice or macaroni
vepřové – pork
  vepřová pečeně se zelím a knedlíky – roast pork with boiled cabbage and dumplings in a rich gravy
  šunka po staročesku – boiled ham old-Czech style with plum sauce, prunes, walnut and kernels, served in a wine sauce
  vepřové žebírko – pork chops
  vepřový řízek – the Czech version of Wiener schnitzel
zajíc – hare

FISH

humr or mořský rak – lobster or crayfish
kapr – carp
  kapr vařeny s máslem – boiled carp in melted butter
  kapr pečený – grilled carp
kaviár – caviar
krevety – prawns
losos – salmon
platýs – flounder
ryba – fish

pstruh – trout
pstruh pečený – grilled trout
rybí filé – fish fillet, usually cod
sardinky – sardines
sled – herring
slaneček – salted herring
štika – pike
treska – cod
úhoř – eel
ústřice – oysters
uzená – kipper

HERBS, PULSES AND VEGETABLES
zelenina – vegetables
brambory – potatoes
    hranolky – French fries
celer – celery
červená řepa – beetroot
česnek – garlic
chřest – asparagus
čočka – lentil
cibule – onions
fazole – beans
houby – mushrooms
hrášek – peas
květák – cauliflower
kaštan – chestnut
knedlíky – dumplings
kyselé zelí – sauerkraut
mrkev – carrots
obloha – pickled vegetables
okurka – cucumber
paprika – peppers
petržel – parsley
rajská jablíčka – tomatoes
ředkvička – radish
salát – salad
    hlávkový salát – mixed green
        salad
    okurkový salát – cucumber
        salad
    fazolový salát – bean salad
    salát z červené řepy –
        beetroot salad
špenát – spinach
zelí – cabbage

DESSERTS
moučníky – desserts
cukrovi – biscuits or cookies
dort – cake or tart
čokoládový dort – chocolate cake
jablka v županu – apple baked in
    flaky pastry and stuffed with
    raisins, sugar and cinnamon
jablkový závin/strudel – apple
    strudel, usually with a topping
    of whipped cream
kompot – stewed fruit
livance – sweet blinis with jam
omeleta se zavařěninou – jam
    omelette
palačinky – pancakes
rýžový nákyp – rice pudding
smetana - cream
švestkové knedlíky – plum
    dumplings
zmrzlína – ice cream

SÝRY (CHEESES)
eidam – edam
gouda as in English
niva – roquefort

OVOCE (FRUIT)
ananas – pineapple
banány – bananas
borůvky – bilberries
broskve – peaches
brusinky – cranberries
citróny – lemons
hrozny – grapes
hrušky – pears
jablka – apples
jahody – strawberries
maliny – raspberries
pomeranč – orange
švestky – plums
třešně – cherries

DRINKS
Becherovka – sweetish herb
    liqueur made in Karlovy Vary,
    served cold; may be drunk as
    an aperitif

Borovická – fiery juniper-flavoured spirit
čaj – tea
káva – coffee
mléko – milk
pivo – beer (*světlé, černé/tmávé* – light/dark)
slivovice – plum brandy
vino – wine (*bílé/cervené* – white/red)
voda – water (*minerálka* – mineral water)

WHITE WINES

Rulandské Bilé (Pinot Blanc) – dry with an almondish aroma, is quite reliable and improves with ageing.

Rulandské Šedé (Pinot Gris) – a light subdued wine that brings out the flavour of chicken and beef dishes

Rýnský Ryzlink (Rhenish Riesling) – a light, spicy number, full-bodied if a little sour

Ryzling Vlašsky – used to make the highly palatable sparkling wine known as Bohemia Sekt

Tramín – full-bodied and tangy with a perfumed aroma

Veltlinské Zelené – a cousin of the Austrian favourite Grüner Veltliner. This very drinkable wine, light and fresh with a hint of spice, goes down a treat with fish and vegetable dishes

RED WINES

Frankovka – a regular on Czech wine lists, this full-bodied red goes well with game

Portugalské Modré (Blue Portugal) – ruby in colour with a smooth, aromatic texture and less tannic than many similar wines

Rulandské Červené (Pinot Noir) – highly rated by wine connoisseurs, this full-bodied red is not dissimilar to a Burgundy

Vavřinecké/Svatovavřinecké – a little tannic for some tastes, this highly serviceable red is a popular choice with Czech diners

Recipes

Fruit dumplings

800g potatoes	
2 eggs	
1 tsp salt	
200g flour	
100g semolina	
1tsp cinnamon	
100g sugar	
12 plums	
100g fresh bread crumbs	
80g butter or margarine	

Boil the potatoes, allow them to cool, then peel and grate them into a large bowl. Sift the flour on to the potatoes, then add the semolina and salt and mix well. Beat the eggs and fold them into the mixture to make a smooth dough.

In a small bowl mix the cinnamon and sugar together. Remove the stones from the plums and put a teaspoon of the spicy sugar mix into the centre of each plum.

Knead the dough and roll it out on a well-floured board, to a thickness of 2cm. Cut into 12 squares, then place one plum on each square of dough and fold it up round the plum to form a sealed ball. Cook for 15 minutes in boiling water.

Brown the bread-crumbs by frying them in butter. When the dumplings are cooked, drain them well, before rolling them in the breadcrumbs. Serve hot with whipped cream or melted butter.

▲ Plum dumplings with poppy seeds

▲ Potato pancakes with smoked pork and sauerkraut

Potato pancakes

675g potatoes
200g plain flour
2 eggs
1 onion
150ml milk
25g butter or margarine
salt and pepper to season
50g grated cheese (optional)

Chop the onions finely, then melt some of the butter in a saucepan and sauté the pieces until soft. Boil the potatoes, allow to cool, then peel and grate. Mix together with the onions and the flour. Beat the eggs into the milk. Make a well in the centre of the potato and slowly pour the milk and eggs into the mixture, stirring well to make a thick, creamy batter (add extra milk if necessary). Season with salt and pepper.

Melt the rest of the butter in a shallow, heavy frying pan. Spoon some of the mixture into the pan so it spreads thinly across the bottom. Cook the pancake for a few minutes until it's golden brown underneath. Free the edge of the pancake with a spatula, then turn it over and lightly brown the other side. Repeat with the rest of the mixture.

To serve with an optional cheese topping, roll the pancakes and place them in a shallow baking tray. Sprinkle with grated cheese and grill lightly until the cheese melts.

Published by Thomas Cook Publishing
Thomas Cook Holdings Ltd
PO Box 227
Thorpe Wood
Peterborough PE3 6PU
United Kingdom

Telephone: 01733 503571
Email: books@thomascook.com

ISBN 1 841570 59 1

Distributed in the United States of
America by the Globe Pequot Press,
PO Box 480, Guilford, Connecticut
06437, USA

Publisher: Donald Greig
Commissioning Editor: Deborah Parker
Map Editor: Bernard Horton

Project management: Dial House
    Publishing
Series Editor: Christopher Catling
Copy Editor: Lucy Thomson
Proofreader: Jan Wiltshire

Series and cover design: WhiteLight
Cover artwork: WhiteLight and
    Kaarin Wall
Text layout: SJM Design Consultancy,
    Dial House Publishing
Maps prepared by Polly Senior
    Cartography

Repro and image setting: PDQ Digital
    Media Solutions Ltd
Printed and bound in Italy by
    Eurografica SpA

Written and researched by: **Chris and
    Melanie Rice**

We would like to thank Caroline Jones for
the photographs used in this book, to
whom the copyright belongs, with the
exception of the following:
Ted Hardin (page 3)
Neil Setchfield (page 62).

The contents of this book are believed to
be correct at the time of printing.
Establishments may open, close or change
and Thomas Cook Holdings Ltd cannot
accept responsibility for errors or
omissions, or for the consequences of any
reliance on the information provided.
Descriptions and assessments are given in
good faith but are based on the authors'
views and experience at the time of
writing and therefore contain an element
of subjective opinion which may not
accord with the reader's subsequent
experiences. The opinions in this book do
not necessarily represent those of
Thomas Cook Holdings Ltd.